PENGUIN BOOKS

A PREPARATION FOR DEA

A Preparation for Death

GREG BAXTER

PENGUIN BOOKS

PENGUIN BOOKS

Published by the Penguin Group
Penguin Books Ltd, 80 Strand, London WC2R 0RL, England
Penguin Group (USA), Inc., 375 Hudson Street, New York, New York 10014, USA
Penguin Group (Canada), 90 Eglinton Avenue East, Suite 700, Toronto, Ontario, Canada M4P 2Y3
(a division of Pearson Penguin Canada Inc.)
Penguin Ireland, 25 St Stephen's Green, Dublin 2, Ireland
(a division of Penguin Books Ltd)
Penguin Group (Australia), 250 Camberwell Road, Camberwell, Victoria 3124, Australia
(a division of Pearson Australia Group Pty Ltd)
Penguin Books India Pvt Ltd, 11 Community Centre, Panchsheel Park, New Delhi – 110 017, India
Penguin Group (NZ), 67 Apollo Drive, Rosedale, Auckland 0632, New Zealand
(a division of Pearson New Zealand Ltd)
Penguin Books (South Africa) (Pty) Ltd, 24 Sturdee Avenue, Rosebank, Johannesburg 2196, South Africa

Penguin Books Ltd, Registered Offices: 80 Strand, London WC2R 0RL, England

www.penguin.com

First published by Penguin Ireland 2010
Published in Penguin Books 2011
1

Copyright © Greg Baxter, 2010
All rights reserved

The moral right of the author has been asserted

Printed in England by Clays Ltd, St Ives plc

ISBN: 978-0-141-04844-4

www.greenpenguin.co.uk

Penguin Books is committed to a sustainable
future for our business, our readers and our
planet. This book is made from paper certified
by the Forest Stewardship Council.

For Walter

He remembers being born somewhere, having believed in native errors,
having proposed principles and preached inflammatory stupidities.
He blushes for it . . . and strives to abjure his past, his real or imaginary
fatherlands, the truths generated in his very marrow. He will find peace
only after having annihilated in himself the last reflex of the citizen, the
last inherited enthusiasm . . . The man who can no longer take sides
because all men are necessarily right and wrong, because everything is at
once justified and irrational – that man must renounce his own name,
tread his identity underfoot, and begin a new life in impassibility or
despair.

E. M. Cioran, *A Short History of Decay*

Contents

Preface

In August 2007, I found myself alone in a house I did not want in one of the bland boomtime estates of north Dublin. My marriage had ended. This book is mostly the story of what came after. I shall try to explain a few things, here, about what came before.

I arrived in Ireland in 2003. I'd been living in Baton Rouge, Louisiana, the few years previous to that, writing a novel. When the book failed to sell, I decided to leave the US for Europe: I could not bear the humiliation of being an unpublished novelist in a country where bad writing, as it seemed to me, had become institutionalized. I resented everyone I knew – for their success, which I considered fraudulent, or for their stupidity, which I considered implacable.

In Dublin, I was unemployed for seven months. During this period I revised the novel. I walked from the house I was sharing to a shopping centre down the road, where there was a small café that was never crowded. I plugged in my laptop and worked. I remember very little specifically about this time. I only remember that on the day I finished the revisions, I felt happy. The book had doubled in size, but I had, inarguably, dealt with every criticism it had received. It now answered everyone's concerns. When I went up to pay, I informed the owner that I'd been working on my novel, and was finished, and I wanted to thank him personally for giving me the space. In front of other patrons, he screamed at me for using up his electricity without permission, and only drinking coffee when everyone else ate. He told me never to come back. It was not too long after this that I realized the revision of that novel had been a waste of time: all I had done was glue, clumsily, a great deal of conventionality around a book I believed was original.

Eventually I got a job as a reporter on a weekly newspaper for doctors. This was a job I was not qualified for and did not want, yet I remain there today. I have tried quitting – serving verbal notice twice – and I have tried to get promotions, but my attempts at both were always half-hearted, and I always botched them.

For about a year I worked very hard at becoming a good reporter. I did not want to become a good reporter, but I felt I ought to become good at something. I wrote a second novel, which an agent didn't like, and I gave up trying to sell it before I had to face any more rejection. I realized that being a good reporter was not – to me – its own reward, and when I was passed over for an important promotion I felt I deserved, I saw my life heading toward an unbearable and unending monotony. Shortly after that, I spotted an ad for a job teaching evening creative writing courses at the Irish Writers' Centre. I applied, and got the job. I did not know that getting this job was to become the most significant event in my life.

I knew well from past experience that people who call themselves writers, and who teach creative writing, usually divorce creativity from learning. They prioritize writing over reading. I wanted to avoid this at all costs. I had no intention of teaching courses in which adults sat around taking blind stabs at creativity. I wanted to introduce students to the value of reading, and thinking about, great literature. I wanted them to understand that their lives were not sufficient preparation for writing, and that the desire to be a writer was not the same as writing. I had gone about becoming a writer in the worst way – with greed and overconfidence – and I suppose I wanted to teach patience and learning as a form of penance. But I achieved more than that: I discovered a little honesty within myself. I put a lot of effort into a rediscovery of literature that allowed me to admire books that jealousy and pettiness had required me to scorn. Most of my students arrived hoping to become fiction writers. But my new interest in honesty compelled me to introduce autobiography: I had them read Montaigne, Augustine and Seneca, along with some more recent masters. I asked them to tell the truth about themselves, because that's what I was trying to do, and I needed to talk about it constantly. I began to write some true stories of my own.

In those evenings I discovered, at long last, a part of me that was honest, and I began to resent the rest of my life for the dishonesty required to get through it. So, around December 2006, I began a campaign of personal sabotage (or rather, I intensified a campaign that had begun much earlier). I fell asleep on friends in bars. I began to drink in the mornings. I didn't come home some nights. In February 2007, I bought that house in north Dublin, and further entrenched myself in a life I wanted to obliterate. In order to express my resentment for buying the house, I hardly ever came home. I bought a Vespa to get around town more easily – I had taken on three classes a week now, and was drinking after every one – and avoided the fact that my life was heading in two opposite directions.

Once my marriage was over and I was alone in the house –
from August onward – a curious thing happened. Selfishness – or
at least the kind of selfishness whose outward expression is the
whining and childish jeremiad that had become the mode of my
existence – seemed totally pointless. To whom would I express
my selfishness? On whom would I take out my frustrations? I
couldn't leave Ireland, because I owed the bank half a million
euro for a house that was worth far less than that, and thus unsell-
able. I started teaching four nights a week, and I wrote in the
empty spaces of time I found around and within the act of living
the story – late nights, lunchtimes, early mornings.

Traditional autobiography is composed after the experience
has passed. I wrote this book in the very panic of the experiences
that inspired it. It reaches into memory and the past, but it is a
constant rush into the darkness of the undiscovered. There was
never an end in sight, until I landed in it. I was living a hectic life,
and I presumed I would simply have a heart attack and die before
the question of an end arose. That is not exaggeration – in fact,
the urgency with which I pursued honesty is, in every sentence
of this book, a preparation for death. Nevertheless, the story had
momentum, because the annihilation of ambition and entitle-
ment is a process that deepens. You think you've told an
eviscerating truth about yourself, but all you've done is discover
the lie that it was founded on, so you tell a new truth, and so on,
until there are no guts left to rip out. And that is the end.

I

Two Working Days

I

On a rainy/sunny afternoon in mid-March 2007, I met Evelyn, a student, for lunch at Thomas Read's, a pub not far from my office. She had been in New York the previous week to celebrate her twenty-ninth birthday.

I got there early and ordered a bottle of red wine – the cheapest. The wine was warm and sour. I thought it might be corked, but what if it weren't, and another bottle came that was the same? The pub was mildly busy. It's a pleasant place to eat lunch, with big windows over Dame and Parliament streets, and you can watch the dense and aggravated flow of cars and buses and foot traffic. I chose a seat at the back, in the raised area, so we wouldn't be spotted.

At a quarter past one, Evelyn arrived. She is tall with dark brown hair, and sleepy and inconclusive blue-brown eyes. She has small breasts and broad shoulders, a tiny waist, and long arms and legs and fingers. She slipped easily into the scene, with the elegance, almost a shyness, of those women who can hide in dark restaurants, walk invisibly around the city, and sleep through afternoons in hotels.

We finished the wine and ordered another bottle. It was as

sour as the previous, but by then it didn't matter. When my food came – cod and chips – I didn't want to eat. My gut was a derelict mill. Some days it was hot and murky; on others, a dry wind blew through it. Nothing stayed put for long: I didn't seem to *process* anything. I just ate and ran to the toilet. Over the previous six or eight weeks, I'd dropped ten pounds. My face had turned a shade or two greyer – I looked like a jar of old rainwater – and I had no energy. It wasn't just the late nights during the week, though that was surely most of it. That January I'd been struck by glandular fever, and ignored it to save sick days for hangovers. Three months later the glands in my armpits were still like soft oranges.

Evelyn got a plate of pasta and finished half of it with a scowl. She was living a secret life that involved two men, and I found her to be the most intriguing person I had ever met. She seemed a little shocked that she was twenty-nine.

She talked about New York: museums she visited, restaurants and hotels. Her favourite spot was the Strand Bookstore; she spent hours in the section for rare and first edition books. She had one with her – a gift for me – and we sniffed it: that's exactly what the whole place smelled like, she said. Her mother, who had never left Ireland before, was with her in New York. They took the subway everywhere, which terrified the mother: the lurking and shadowy implication of murder, the violence of crowds and ethnicity.

By the time lunch ended, I was drunk again. We stood outside the pub for a moment and, to avoid being jostled by pedestrians, we stood very close together. Evelyn was drunk too. She tried to convince me to skip work and come with her to the Irish Film Institute, but taking the afternoon off would have meant quitting my job, and I wasn't quite ready to do that. We casually discussed the possibility that we might meet later that night.

I watched her disappear around the corner. Most women just walk away, but a few, like Evelyn, can vanish; and when they vanish, you watch the absence of them. I decided I needed quite a few cigarettes and a coffee and some chewing gum. At once I regretted my decision not to go to the cinema. I felt that if we'd stayed together for a few more hours, we would've got on a plane to Paris. In the little shop two doors down, I dropped change and must have looked like a clown, trying to gather it. I was surrounded by the naked calves of office girls and solicitors in high heels. It does not take too many naked calves to make one feel surrounded by them. I wanted to lick them. I often feel one drink away from whatever makes a dog hump women's legs.

The walk from Dame Street and Temple Bar to my office on Upper Ormond Quay takes you from a city – at least in daytime – that is clean and full of quirky cafés and small art galleries and oinking tourists to one that is grimy and dilapidated and full of lawyers and criminals and addicts orbiting the Four Courts. The Liffey is always murky and snotty, and if you are not feeling well it makes you want to vomit. And if the river does not make you want to vomit, then look along the quays, upon the sad and unambitious architecture of the city, and you will want to vomit. I got myself a coffee at a little soup place owned by two nice black-haired women, whom I suspect/hope are lovers. It is nice to have romance around. I spat out my gum and drank about half the coffee – I needed to be slightly alert – and smoked another cigarette, and by then my gut felt like an agitated beehive so I walked to the little crumbling potholed alley that lies behind my office building, where heroin addicts crawl harmlessly into shadowy garageways and shoot up, and I puked for a little while.

The puking made me weak, and the walk up one flight of stairs to my desk left me breathless. I was very late. One of my bosses came out to glare at me – as though I would become so frightened by him that I'd never take a lunch again. I waved and burped. I sat at my desk and moved my mouse to wake up the screen. I entered my password. I watched as my email refreshed. Press releases, doctors complaining, spam, breaking news reports, on and on and on. Every hour of every day.

I put on my headphones and hoped a text would come from Evelyn. One did. She said she wished we could've spent the afternoon together. I imagined her sitting somewhere in the back of a large empty cinema watching a subtitled Korean masterpiece with fighting and star-crossed lovers, and I went into the bathroom to masturbate. I had never done that before, and I went with trepidation. The problem, of course, is that once you find a comfortable spot, there's no end to it. Pretty soon you go there just because you're bored. Pretty soon it's like a cigarette break. But I could not shake the image: Evelyn, on my lap in the back row of the cinema, holding onto the seat in front of her, watching the film, fucking me. I couldn't sit down. The toilet seat was too disgusting, and the thought that anyone in my office had settled down there for a long and stinky shit was ghastly. The whole thing was ghastly (there was also a brown toilet brush on the floor), but I could not stop. Now I saw myself between her legs, masticating with bovine stupidity and single-mindedness. And she could not stop coming. I stood straight up in the tiny little room and yanked at myself for five minutes, until I was too exhausted to continue.

I had a cigarette to catch my breath afterward, out in our grey little parking square. It was the only way I could breathe. Nobody ever cleans the space – though every week someone empties the big dumpster – and ten years or more of cigarettes and muck have accumulated in the corners. Every year the office forms a committee to clean it up – and every year the committee gets a different name – but nobody joins it.

I left the office at five and walked toward a pub for a few drinks on my own; the friends I was to meet weren't coming in for a while. The cars on the quays had thirty minutes of gridlock to face before they reached O'Connell Bridge, which was less than half a mile away. Girls in suits and runners pounded up and down the footpaths. Tourists were lost – nobody came that way on purpose. The days were getting longer in a hurry. Summer was coming – there was no way back.

I sat at the bar and ordered a beer. I took out a book – the one from Evelyn – and smelled it again: the scent of long-dead and forgotten authors. I imagined her on the floor, between high shelves, the tops of which you have to reach with ladders, surrounded by too many books to carry back to Ireland. She would buy them all. They would reappear in her bedroom. They would watch her slip into and out of her dressing gown. They would sleep beside her – she would read them until her eyes closed. At work, as she absent-mindedly filled out spreadsheets and calculated year-end whatevers, she would miss them, and daydream, and want to write her own.

II

Whenever I cover stories outside the office, I like to procrastinate in the city. Other journalists hail taxis while jotting down notes on their notes, or jog back to their computers while the memories are still fresh, but I take circuitous walks, window shop, browse bookstores. In April – it might have been May – I sat through a four-hour conference on healthcare in the Conrad Hotel. I had been out very late the previous night, so I hid in the back rows unshaven and smelling of sweet cheese and nicotine and sent texts to all the people I'd been with to blame them for my hangover. Now and again I'd write down something that was said by a man addressing the crowded room. He would say something like: The more money *I* make, the better patients feel. And everyone would clap like seals at a zoo.

I skipped the free lunch, roast chicken – who would I sit with, and what would we talk about? – and made my way through Stephen's Green. The morning had been bright and warm, but by the time I left the conference the day had come down cold and soapy, and it was beginning to rain. A few black umbrellas emerged from and disappeared into the trees. The rain was falling softly into the treetops and loudly into the little ponds. My bag was heavy. I had crammed a lot of books into it that morning – I never know what mood I will be in – assuming the weather would hold and I could grab a little sunlit patch of grass and read for an hour or two. But I was happier this way. For my first two years in Ireland, the rain depressed me. Now, whenever it is warm and agreeable, I lie around dreaming of grey skies and wind and short days in December.

I stopped in to McDaid's – a regular spot for me – and took a seat at a stool in the window, where I could watch the rain intensify and bash the little alleyway between the Westbury and Bruxelles. The glass was fogged at the four corners. Nobody knew then that we were headed for the rainiest summer in a hundred years. I ordered a pint of Guinness. I only drink Guinness when I want to avoid becoming unreasonably drunk.

There was one man at the bar, a big black man in a Nike tracksuit and bling sunglasses – surely a Westbury resident – and a white-haired couple at one of the small tables in the very back. The television was showing rugby, a repeat from the southern hemisphere, and only the bartender, who looked much like Anthony Perkins in *Psycho*, but shorter, with a more pronounced chin, was watching, and only then from time to time. The black man, an American, drank a gin and tonic and said things about the music industry – who was who in New York, LA, etc., and old stories about people he considered legends. The bartender, the only person to whom he could possibly have been speaking, agreed in nods but had nothing to add. Two German girls came in and sat at the short side of the bar, their backs directly to mine, and when the cold blew in the black man said, *Merry Christmas, motherfucker!* to no one in particular. Outside, tourists in bright jackets and hoods stopped to consider McDaid's and Bruxelles, wondering if they were restaurants, if they might find some Irish stew and soda bread.

I placed my books on the ledge in front of the window – one was the book Evelyn had brought back from New York, which I always carried with me. I wanted to reread the stories we'd be talking about in class that night. My pint came. It was a cold glass and the head had spilled over the sides, and it was pleasant to behold. I took a sip immediately.

I opened two of the books – Mansfield and Hemingway. I teach 'The Daughters of the Late Colonel' and, depending on my mood, any number of Hemingway stories; that evening I'd be teaching 'A Clean, Well-Lighted Place'. I took my notebook out in order to write a few things I wanted to say about them. But this seemed to desecrate the calm of the moment so I decided to write nothing.

I turned to find the black guy staring at me. He said something like, Shit, how many books are you reading?

I moved so he could see them better.

That's a lot of motherfucking reading. You teach?

Yeah, I said.

All fucking right, he said – I remember he said that. He went back to his gin and tonic. He had nothing with him. No reading. No phone. He just seemed to want to stir his straw and now and again take a drink, but not get drunk. I waited a moment and went back to my pint.

Resentment, if you let it, will weave itself into your DNA, and replicate. Every cell in your body becomes it. You feel nothing authentically, and, if you are a writer, you produce reactionary trash. You must let go of the desire to bring down the society you loathe. You must learn to discard any hope of making a difference. You must stop asking dumb questions.

I want to think quietly, calmly, spaciously, never to be interrupted, never to have to rise from my chair, to slip easily from one thing to another, without any sense of hostility, or obstacle. [Woolf]

When I think of growing, it is in a lowly way, with a constrained and cowardly growth, strictly for myself. [Montaigne]

What I like about Dudley and some of the others is that they know enough not to want to do a stroke of honest work . . . Sink or swim is their motto. They look at their fathers and grandfathers, all brilliant successes in the world of American flapdoodle. They prefer to be shitheels, if they have to be. [Miller]

I had become a resentful and jealous and desperate would-be writer in Louisiana, and I was that same man in Ireland. I woke every morning at dawn and put on three or four layers and a winter hat and bashed revisions into my first book. And when that failed I bashed a second book into existence. No thought I had was quiet. Everything was a military march. I could not imagine a fate of anonymity – life was meaningless without impact. I believed that I could alter society. How pathetic that self seems to me now.

It is enough for me to hear someone talk sincerely about ideals, about the future, about philosophy, to hear him say 'we' with a certain inflection of assurance, to hear him invoke 'others' and regard himself as their interpreter – for me to consider him my enemy. [Cioran]

Before I found work at the paper, I took on a contract job that was humiliating and paid nothing. I listened to taped speeches and phone conversations and transcribed them. Because I type with four fingers, it took me hours to transcribe a few minutes' worth of tape. And my work was so mistake-riddled that I was invariably docked twenty per cent of my pay. It was mainly corporate work, and often the voices were inaudible – French accents (it was a French company), bad tapes, words I had never heard of. I was like Akaky Akakievich, just *copying*. The guy who served as a kind of boss would call me every fifteen minutes asking how I was getting along. I told him I would be going a lot faster if he stopped calling me every fifteen minutes. He would laugh but he would call me fifteen minutes later. Apparently his other transcribers could type. In four months I probably made two hundred euro. I should have quit, but I needed the money – any amount was better than nothing. And I was writing my novel, which was going to be great, and revolutionize fiction, so I figured I had dignity. A man who believes in his own inviolability can withstand any cruelty, every form of humiliation imaginable.

By the time I gave up the desire to write books that would annihilate society – which was nothing more than the desire to write myself back into society – I had almost nothing left of myself. I wasn't a writer at all, just a slave to my own preoccupation with people who were published.

I got another pint. I felt unusually tipsy and wanted a cigarette. I had set my phone to silent but I could see that the screen was flashing. It was work. I needed to get moving soon.

All the successful journalists I know have one thing in common: they become excited by news, and when there is none of it, they are lost. When they have a story to write, they rush to write it. Their hearts will explode if they don't. I, on the other hand, feel nothing but monotony. But after seven months of unemployment, you capitulate to monotony. No matter how much you might loathe an honest day's work, no matter how little you want to be on phones or sitting through press conferences and writing down every infuriating detail of things that do not matter, you want that pay cheque. You want a drink or some new shoes, or some socks without holes in them. A bottle of wine that does not taste like vinegar. A steak you don't have to stew four hours to make tender. A new winter coat.

After three years of working as a journalist, my life had become a junkyard of comforts. It must be true that to many – to all but a few – this junkyard is the meaning of life. Otherwise the fabric would collapse. If there were not people whose whole life was an Audi, or toilet-roll holders, or a television, or fancy lampshades, or an expensive birthday party for their four-year-old, civilization would end today, this minute.

My pint was finished. The black man was flirting with the German girls. My phone flashed again and I took the call. The news editor asked how the conference had gone. I said it had gone well. Anything front page? Oh, definitely. The rain was the same. I had no umbrella and no waterproof jacket, so the walk to the quays was going to be wet, and for the rest of the afternoon I'd be sitting in an uncomfortable puddle at my desk.

I put the books back into my bag and threw the bag over my shoulder – it seemed heavier now after two pints. The black guy gave me a nod. Earlier, the white-haired man from the back had walked out, rapping his knuckle on the bar as he went. Perhaps they had held a conversation earlier, or maybe they knew each other from the Westbury. Anyway, I had the feeling they didn't expect to see each other again. The black man told the white-haired man to take it easy. The white-haired man told him to do the same. The black guy said, Ain't nothing else *to* do.

I stepped out and stood in the rain. Why hurry when it would not make a difference? No matter what I did, I was going to get wet.

2

That Lovely Season Now Expired

In the summer of 2000, when I was twenty-five and unfathom-
able to myself, I drove with a friend, Brent Benoit, from Baton
Rouge to the Sewanee Writers' Conference at the University of
the South, in Tennessee, where I hoped to announce myself to
the world of Southern letters.

Brent came by my house at seven in the morning. He had
rented a lollipop-red Jeep Cherokee while his truck was in the
shop. It took me half an hour to get out of the house. I had been
out the night before and run into some girlfriends of friends.
They were all beautiful, and I was only beginning to understand
the dangers of being around beautiful women when you are so
full of yourself. I was hungover, and so was Brent, and when we
set off we were both green and quiet. Because it was July, it was
already too hot to think, and we were good enough friends not
to need chit-chat.

Brent and I were studying in the writing programme at Louisiana State University. I was getting along nicely– a few publications,
some awards – and at that time Brent was the only other writer at
LSU who I felt had a chance. He was a big fan of Hemingway and
Faulkner, and he wrote like a great black river splashing out of its

banks. He couldn't spell, and he had no idea what a comma was, but he could write. We had sort of pledged allegiance to each other – we believed we were on similar ascensions – and although we didn't say it, we saw the trip as a pilgrimage.

We bought a loaf of bread, sliced cheese, ham, mayonnaise, a carton of cigarettes, some Kodiak chewing tobacco, and a few cases of beer. We were going to drive the whole way drunk. We had no interest in contemplative dialogues on Art. We wanted nothing more than the raw mayhem of existence. The only difference between us was that his mayhem took the form of constant awe and wonder; mine was venom.

Brent wasn't one of those Southern writers who glorify stereotypes and gaze at the navel of place-ness. But he was comfortable in the landscape, and his characters were very much of the places he wrote about. I, meanwhile, was fundamentally unhappy. Sometimes when I remember the unhappiness I felt at twenty-five, I can't imagine why I didn't kill myself. I sensed that I was an outcast everywhere. My characters were all exiles, and I hated them. In writing, Brent became fulfilled. I just felt eviscerated.

By the time we crossed into Mississippi, we were awake and drunk and listening to music. We sank heavily into the landscape, the crumbling interstates, the dense piney highwaysides to Biloxi that broke expansively at exits, which were all the same, and full of romantic gloominess – grim hotels, food for gluttons, shopping for the poor. We drove it all with the windows down. In Meridian, Mississippi, we passed a chicken warehouse that made me never want to eat a chicken again – a hangar-like structure without walls, right on the side of the interstate, with giant fans propelling a breeze through a hundred shelves of stuffed-full cages. Although the chickens were too cramped to move, they struggled nevertheless, and white feathers floated over the town. In Alabama, we bought some net-backed hats and put on some fake redneck teeth Brent had bought back home, and were given threatening stares at a truck stop.

The easiest way to drive to Sewanee, if you come from the west, is to overshoot it by a hundred miles on the interstate, get to Chattanooga, and take an easy two-lane highway back. But we were sick of interstates and running very late, so we got off and headed straight north, out of Alabama, through back roads of mountains and the Tennessee River valley. I had assumed it would be a lot like the set of *Deliverance*, that I would spot children with eyes in their nostrils and gills in their ankles. But the little towns we passed were just like everywhere else we'd passed: poor, boring. The scenery was nice but the mountains were really just hills, nothing special.

On the long straightaways I got the truck up to a hundred, where it rose dangerously high off the surface of the road and swayed about like a balloon, and going up the switchback roads I had it fishtailing. When I swerved to avoid an eighteen-wheeler coming down the mountain, nearly causing the Jeep to tumble into the woody drop-off beside the road like something from a movie, Brent told me to slow down or he was going to kill me. He was green and I believed him. But we were getting close to Sewanee, and I felt my whole life wrenched forward by the force of my fate. I sensed that I had lifelong friends to meet, and great books ahead of me. I could feel the presence of Barry Hannah, the only living writer I considered a hero, as though the trees and rocks and little streams were whispering clamorously about him.

We arrived late, and had missed the opening reading by the playwright Romulus Linney. We parked at the main reading venue, a small banquet hall at the edge of campus. A group of white-haired and weathered figures were standing around look-ing like Southern writers. If you've ever seen a group of them together, you know what I mean. The closest I can come to describing it accurately is a highbrow and slightly effeminate fishing trip. We asked them where the restaurant was and got an incredulous stare. One asked, Have you *only* just arrived? We told him we had driven from Louisiana that morning. We were beat, and we had hauled ass. Instead of giving us directions, he told us we had wasted our whole trip missing Linney and might as well go home. We waited a moment, until we realized he wasn't joking and that he wasn't going to tell us where the restaurant was.

We found it ourselves – it was a two-minute drive around the corner – but as we rushed in, smelling like thirteen hours of driving drunk, everyone was getting up and all the food was being cleared. There was no sign of Barry Hannah, who had just gone through chemotherapy for lymphoma and, I would learn, ate nothing but pink medicinal shakes through a straw. (I had met him a year earlier, before the chemotherapy, in Baton Rouge, when he sat down with some of the students at LSU to talk about his writing.) We got something to eat only because Dave Smith, a regular Sewanee conference faculty member, convinced the staff to leave some scraps out for us. Dave was my advisor at LSU and my boss at the *Southern Review*, and very much a father figure, whom I admired because of his own venom and followed like a disciple. This meant, of course, that our future held the inevita-bility of disappointment, of neither of us measuring up, which is how all my relationships, every one of them, even with Brent, have ended since that trip to Tennessee.

That first night, after a short meet-and-greet at the main house, the nighthawks of the conference retreated to Rebel's Rest, a large, old log cabin situated in the midst of a vast green lawn, for drinks. We met Marc and Adam, two writers in their early thirties who weren't from the South, who seemed like pretty cool dudes, and when a little weasel-of-a-poet kicked us out at midnight, we stole a bunch of cans and drank on the street until four a.m. Drinking on the street in Sewanee is a serious offence, we would learn, and over the rest of the ten days we were frequently chased around the campus by university police and ratted upon by the kinds of people who saw our behaviour as a disgrace to the cause of art and decency. Rather than try to win toleration, we started a sort of parallel conference with a few like-minded young guys. Brent was more charming about it, so I was singled out as the Bad Seed. It was easy to single me out – not just because I was dislikable, but because I was the nobodiest of nobodies. Within a couple of days, the conference organizer wouldn't even speak to me, since I was sleeping through all the nine a.m. readings, or missing them and going straight to Rebel's Rest for midday Bloody Marys and beer, and to talk to Barry, who sat on the back porch chain-smoking and reading.

We met officially in the workshop he was co-teaching with the experimental writer Padgett Powell, though Barry missed some sessions, including the one in which my story was discussed, because he was so unwell. But at the Rest I sat beside him and listened and drank. Sometimes there were a lot of us, sometimes just a few. He made no sense – he spoke like a character in one of his stories, the kind of man who says he is *crucified by the truth*. These were not conversations but officiations of his wisdoms, sometimes profound, sometimes ludicrous, and often repetitive, but what did I care? The other writers, obsessed with status, treated me with loathing and suspicion. (William Gay was also friendly, but nobody could understand him at all.)

Around the university campus, there were long and peaceful trails through the woods. I imagine it was very tranquil until we got there, a hundred writers, to pervert it. One day a few of us were walking around out of boredom when we came upon a group creeping quietly and reverently through Nature. There is nothing sillier in the universe than an excursion of mediocre Southern poets on a nature trail. You feel as though you have interrupted a dozen unborn compositions exploding sentimentally in their hearts, and there are probably dogs in them, or Confederate ghosts.

There were softball games on a few afternoons, and this was the most popular of all activities. The teams usually fielded something like twenty-five players, which meant that everyone had a zone of about five square feet for which they were responsible, so the outfielders – dozens of them – mostly just stood dozily and watched balls fly over their heads. The dissident wing attended after a few hours at the Rest, by which time I had to close one eye to bat or field; otherwise I would see ten of everything. I narrowly avoided a fist fight when Powell, a writer I admired very much for *Edisto* and *Typical*, but who treated us like insects, knocked into me and the ball fell beside us. There was a lot of laughter from the gallery. We took a long look at each other, Powell and me. He was a bulldog of a man, and if he got his hands on me I was finished. But I could jab and dart. I had the speed and the reach. I'm certain his long look meant: Why are you even here? Mine meant: I had that fly ball. Anyway, what spectacle could have been more absurd than *that* fight?

And if I touched him, I might as well have packed my bags that second. Brent ran over from right field and led me away.

There were readings in the afternoons, by participants, and in the evenings, by faculty. We attended a few afternoon readings, often because someone from our parallel conference was reading, and we went to all the faculty readings (I was alone in my willingness to skip them). Afterwards, drinks and barefaced networking stretched late into the night. Big salivating circles formed around agents and editors. One woman who was publishing a collection of sweet, unremarkable stories – stories for the broken-hearted girl in all of us – had taped a sign to her back that read: *Blurb my book!* Lots of people wrote promissory signatures on her sign. She would get down on all fours so the guys could scribble legibly, and they would make humping noises. (One member of the faculty, we knew, moved aspiring female authors through his bedroom with promises of recommendations and introductions.) When I tried to make conversation, people looked right through me; only when it was discovered that I worked for the *Southern Review* did I gain a little respect. Suddenly people wanted to know things about me. Suddenly my bad habits seemed romantic. Our group of dissidents swelled. We probably had enough for a softball team.

I should have realized, during those ten days in Tennessee, that my failure as a writer was inevitable. Dave Smith had stressed the importance of an awareness of purpose, an acknowledgement of audience. He believed, like his spiritual mentor, Robert Penn Warren, that to write was to commit a moral act, that a poem was a vote. I tried to apply this. I asked of all my stories, Is this moral? I had no idea. Who was I voting for? What were the issues?

I liked Dave. A lot of people in Baton Rouge didn't. He was caustic and impatient, and when he spoke about art, his voice acquired the gravity of a black hole. If you were young and impressionable, and especially if he liked you, you could not escape its pull. At LSU, the position of Dave's protégé was a position of difference, since everyone else in the programme was a protégé of Andrei Codrescu, who was as much rock star as writer, and a strong believer in the principle that more of anything was better, especially writing. Dave would have preferred a world in which ten people wrote. I was seduced by the idea that I might be one of them.

At LSU I had seen Dave as a renegade; now I saw him in his element, among the high priests of a deep-voiced, wrinkled, belligerent tradition. I had duped myself into believing that an apprenticeship could lead to individuality; now I felt less like a protégé and more like a factotum. Two years later I would write the novel only I could write, and he hated it: he told me to begin a new book immediately. I had failed him – as I was always going to, if I was to become myself. He feared that I had grown too insulated, that I was writing for an audience of zero. But what was the alternative? Taping stickers to my back? Fellating editors and agents? Writing books that *suited* people?

Brent was disgusted with the scene as well, but it didn't ruin him. He simply ignored it. He would go on to achieve all that is expected of decent men – have kids, build a business, never stray from his promises, never desire to inflict harm on the weak or insipid or boring or arrogant, or the generous. His books, which have been modest successes, would reveal, through his characters, a humanity in him that I lacked utterly.

*

Seven years later, I am in my dining room in a northern suburb of Dublin, writing. My marriage ended a few months ago. The dining room and living room are at the top of the house, with a little square terrace full of dead plants. One whole side of that top floor is glass, so I can see all of the sky to the south. It's a warm, overcast night, and the light is dwindling out of the clouds. It is also the morning, before work, clear and cool, and the light of the sun, which cleared the horizon only a little while ago, is gathering on the rooftops of my hygienic little estate. It is always something: the weather, morning, night, evening, a weekend. There's nothing to explain. I am writing for nobody. It is only an unbreakable habit.

A week ago I read through some of my old stories, which I wrote around the time I took the trip to Tennessee. Full of desire, of wanting, of an urge to be published, of ambition, there is within them all an explosive *quaintness*. They scored picayune truths. They deferred to bad influence. This is the effect of inclination: it obliterates difference.

I've stopped eating, for the most part. My liver is a brick. I sleep in my clothes. I shave twice a week. I have painful cavities. Maybe I'll be dead in a year. What is the difference? When Priam came for the body of Hector, he told Achilles: *Such is the way the gods spun life for unfortunate mortals, that we live in unhappiness.*

I go to work. I teach writing classes. I drink on my own. I drink with my students after class, because I have exactly one friend left in Ireland, Henrik, and he has a life. I come home and write for nobody, for an audience of zero. I am incompatible with the concept of the future. How do I explain to anyone that such a life, however unsustainable, is my ideal?

A few days ago, coming home from the bar after class,

sometime around midnight, I drove my Vespa to the docks in Ringsend, which is dramatically out of my way, and parked for a while beside my first apartment in Dublin. I used to jog there in the mornings, in the cold and sometimes rain, before the sun came up and the streets filled with traffic, past the toll bridge, beside the sleeping cottages, and I observed the blue mooing of cargo ships, the high clanks of crane activity, the idling of empty trucks. I saw no people. From time to time, through a frosty cottage window, I would be spied by a cat or dog. I ran for thirty minutes, up and down the street, without hope or desire, infinitely nobody.

Each writer at Sewanee got a twenty-minute one-on-one session with a faculty member of his or her choice, and on the third-to-last day of the conference I sat down with Barry. It was about ten in the morning. I was up early that morning with nerves. What did I have to say to him? I was aware that Barry had much more in common with Brent than with me – the humanity and wonder. This didn't unsettle me. I didn't want to be an acolyte, one of the so-called Sons of Barry. I was happy just to hang with the man who wrote *Ray*, *Airships*, etc.

We discussed my story for a while. We smoked a lot of cigarettes. We talked a bit about William Goyen, whose work I liked very much at the time. He told me to ask him for help, when I got a book together, because he was going to get my ass published, but I think he said that to a lot of people. Inexplicably we got on to the subject of SUVs. He loved them. He said he admired our red Cherokee – which was preposterous but true. He had a green Cherokee of his own and he said he felt like the captain of an aircraft carrier, driving it.

Then he said, I feel like a cheeseburger.

I said, That sounds nice.

He said, You feel like a cheeseburger?

I could eat.

Or do you want to catch the next reading?

I didn't have the heart to tell him I didn't know which reading he meant.

We drove around fairly aimlessly for about an hour, and I got the sense he hadn't really wanted a cheeseburger after all. He just wanted to get away. We stopped at a gas station for cigarettes, and we loitered there a long time, since he said he liked to spend time in strange gas stations. He was not the man I had seen once before, at LSU, trim and handsome, with a full head of hair. He was swollen from his therapy, and his skin was pink and raw. His eyes, which were once little black marbles, bulged like eggs. Yet he retained his presence. He started to get worried that I needed a cheeseburger, so he asked some locals if they knew a place – not a drive-through but a diner. It was the experience of a cheeseburger he sought. They gave us complex directions, so he bought me some beef jerky and himself a fountain coke, but he couldn't drink it.

You want to go back? he asked.

Not really, I said.

All right, he said – and he had a way of drawing this out, *All right*, which implied that we were going in search of some trouble.

We went to the Army/Navy store, a pilgrimage he made every summer in Sewanee. It was about twenty minutes' drive from the gas station.

I love Army/Navys, he said. I'm fascinated with World War Two. I was born into it, and I feel like I fought it myself.

Yes, I said, though he had told me the exact same thing on two previous occasions.

The way out to the Army/Navy took us down a winding road, and he grew quiet. His smile disappeared. Instead of talking, we watched the landscape roll by. Woods and farms. Patches of traffic in the opposite direction. The day was hazy and warm and bright – even with sunglasses I had my hand above my eyes.

The Army/Navy was all by itself in a gravel parking lot. A few cars were parked in it, but not in rows. You just pulled in and stopped wherever you liked. He killed the engine, but rather than getting out, he sat with his eyes closed and breathed laboriously through his nose. I didn't want to insult him by asking if he was okay. After a few minutes he shook off the nausea and stepped out.

The store might have said Army/Navy, but really it was a white survivalist shop. Knives, firearms, shovels, ammunition, and thousands of Confederate flags. There were some serious rednecks talking to the clerk, and they all looked me up and down – white T-shirt, cargo shorts, flip-flops, fancy chrome sunglasses. I might as well have been black. I got myself a souvenir – a grey NAVY T-shirt. When I went to pay, I found Barry talking to the rednecks. The rednecks were pontificating about the importance of the Confederate battle flag, about the history of the Civil War, the aggression of Federalism. If only they knew who they were talking to – the greatest Southern storyteller since Flannery O'Connor. Barry bought a Confederate flag bandana out of affection for irony.

One redneck said, They're trying to take away our right to fly that. But they can't take our history.

I waited. I wondered if Barry might say to them something like, You are going to waste your life believing in something that

23

owns you; or, Say something wise for once in your life; or, Look what we did, are doing, to this place we pretend to worship; or, Perfect! We knew you'd be like that. These are the things his characters might say. Instead he looked angrily at the man, pointed his finger at the man's bushy moustache (Barry has famous antipathy for the moustache – one always appears on characters he dislikes), and said, *You're goddamned right.*

The redneck took a step back. Barry is five foot nothing, and with cancer very much an old man, but this large Tennessean got out of his way.

We got back in his Cherokee and he closed his eyes again. He asked if I minded driving, because he was not up to it. I couldn't tell him I needed my glasses. I was totally blind to road signs, to distant traffic, to lanes. But I had to drive or we were never leaving. I couldn't figure out how to move the seat back, and he was starting to fade out of consciousness, so I drove in his seat the way he had it. My knees were up around the steering wheel. I kept my elbows very high to avoid my knees, and my face was nearly at the window. I just tried to keep us on the road. When you have bad eyesight, often you don't realize you're blind until you need badly to see something.

After about twenty minutes, Barry woke up and smoked a cigarette. He looked at me with curiosity but said nothing. We spoke a little bit about Europe. He said he liked Paris. I told him I was probably going to leave the US one day, and for good.

Yes, he said. I can understand that.

At the beginning of our drive, he had said something about the daughter of a friend who was shot in a bank during a robbery. She lived, but she would never walk again. I wasn't sure how to respond. Had he known the girl? How close was the friend? We were going through a little spot of earth with a few stores and gas stations – these places are not towns. I said, trying to conjure a little profundity: We are all at the whim of randomness.

Randomness? I withered into myself. He was silent for a few moments, and I felt very stupid. I started to wonder if he might turn back and find someone more interesting. We stopped at the light and he turned to me. He said, Greg, you can't live your life that way. You can't be afraid to leave your house.

When we got back to Rebel's Rest, there was nobody about. Everyone was eating lunch or taking a midday nap. Barry said he needed some sleep. He shook my hand and said, Thanks for our day. Two days later he would inscribe the same thing for me in a copy of one of his books.

I took a seat on the patio and grabbed a beer – even though drinking wasn't allowed at that hour – and smoked a lot of cigarettes on my own. Brent and Marc showed up after a while. They asked if Barry had liked my story, and I said he had, but I'd forgotten almost everything he'd said about it. In any case, I'd forgotten my story. Gradually the dissident wing trickled in. By that point in the conference, we could locate midday drinking by its scent, anywhere on campus. I have a photograph from that afternoon. A woman who had joined us took it, then mailed us copies. In it, we are all pretending not to notice the camera. The day is bright and everyone has a drink in his hand. I am perched on a railing. There are some people beside me. Some others are sitting in chairs. I can see what I am thinking – that I was finally part of something, that I could lead something large and magnificent. That I could annihilate the lukewarm vision of American letters. That by desiring I created – a book, a life, a movement. What a foolish illusion. I spent many years trying to interpret existence, when I ought to have been squandering it. What is there to learn from life, except that it ends, and for a little while you are alive? I could not even, until recently, comprehend the beauty – the unimportance – of my afternoon with Barry, who is still alive, I think, and is pausing to admire strange gas stations, searching for the experience of a cheeseburger, accidentally teaching his own life.

3
The City of Perpetual Night

My grandfather, Herbert Fuchs, was a schoolteacher in Vienna before the Second World War. In July 1944 he was killed by a bomb in a small Carinthian village, a village of no importance, where he was serving as an officer in the Waffen-SS. He never received the letter sent by his wife Maria, my grandmother, with news of the birth of his second son, my father; it was returned unopened not long after Maria received, by post, the notice of his death. She used to tell this story with no emotion, though I am certain that, of her three husbands, Herbert was the only one she loved. In fact, except for Herbert's sister, Erika, nobody has ever told the story of his death with sorrow.

Although I know almost nothing of him, or perhaps because of that, Herbert lurks in the interstices of my life with the tormenting persistence of a sense that you have forgotten something. His death was the first and most drastic accident to turn the accidental course of the world toward my existence. Only something drastic would do. Without Herbert's death, and Maria's emigration to the States to remarry, my mother, who came from Splendora, Texas, would have never met my father at a bus stop in Austin.

Over several years, Maria told me portions of her story before and after the war, in the hope that I'd write it. She did not wish to be preserved forever – she is no egoist – but I think she wanted very much to preserve her memory of Vienna, of Herbert, to fix it in an unalterable state, and leave something for the rest of us, so we would know where we had come from. It is not extraordinary, and there is no wild end to it. There is only the commonplace irony of a crippled mind at the end of a rich history: at the age of eighty-seven, she lives in a nursing home in San Antonio, Texas, as far from her own life as she could ever be, and suffers from vascular dementia. Within her day-to-day pattern, she keeps up with familiar identities and places, but anything outside it – me, for instance – is lost unless it walks right in front of her.

Maria met Herbert in a Viennese military hospital in 1942. She worked as a volunteer nurse, mainly cleaning and re-dressing wounds and keeping soldiers company. He spent weeks there after an artillery shell struck his position: he suffered burns on one half of his body, and his ear was melted off. (When I was younger, I took great pride in a story I must have fabricated, which was that the Russians had cut his ear off to torture him.) They fell in love, I presume, married, and before he was sent back to the war she was pregnant with my father's elder brother, Peter. He would see her once more when Peter was a baby, and when he left again she was pregnant with my father.

It does not strike me as peculiar – never mind that people do such things all the time in war – that Maria, a woman of considerable good looks, would have wasted no time in marrying him. Herbert was handsome in a way – as with all Fuchs men before and after him, he had striking eyes, commanding eyebrows, and a nose like the keel of a boat – and he was rather dashing, especially in uniform. In the pictures I have seen he beholds everything with the aloof confidence of a man who believes he has everything he wants, or knows that by pretending so, he gets what he wants. In the photos that predate Maria, he, usually in a bathing suit, is surrounded by a handful of pretty women; he is lean, muscular, and his legs – he was also an amateur gymnast – are enormous. When he is not around women, he is usually by himself, in hand-some suits, standing in the tipped-hat, hip-forward pose of a rake, usually holding a completely redundant walking stick – a fashion, I hope, of the time. With Maria, in the hospital and later, holding Peter high up in the air, he is a little wiser – more serene than aloof – but very much the same man.

Though his nose was larger than mine – it was truly gigantic – and his chin more square, we look alike, so the thought of what he looked like in Carinthia, dead, commands my attention more and more as I outgrow the age he was. Erika says that only one bomb was dropped, a stray bomb, as though the Allies were simply getting rid of it. Perhaps this is false.

Maria's father owned a taxi company before the war, and as a girl Maria was sent to school with a car and driver. Her father hated Hitler and the Nazis, and blamed them for everything. He foresaw the demise of his country in their takeover. As a result, Maria was against Hitler also – though really (and she has remained this way her whole life) she had no politics at all. Later, like everything else in Austria, her father's business collapsed, and rather than face the ignominy of poverty, embod-ied most painfully in the fact that his daughter might have to walk on her own two feet, he killed himself. She was, I believe, twelve years old.

At the time of the Anschluss, in 1938, Maria was working as a housekeeper and au pair in a large country estate outside Leeds. She was eighteen, and had been there a few years making money and sending it home to her mother. Everybody knew that the annexation of Austria meant war. She was told to mail her passport home at once; there was no such thing as Austria any longer. She should return as soon as her German passport arrived. Maria hated the Germans, and it was disconcerting to find that she was one of them. She has never changed her opinion that Austria and Germany were not just two different countries but two separate civilizations. Germans were sterile mathematicians. They knew nothing of romance and art. They were obedient dogs who ate anything. Even though she held these views, and even though the English family asked her to stay, and even though her mother urged her not to come home, she returned to Vienna.

Herbert's father supported Hitler and the Nazis. Even though he was a doctor – like his father, and his father's father – they were not the kind of people whose children had personal drivers. For most of my life, I had no idea what Herbert's politics were. Maria had never discussed him in that way; perhaps she felt it was none of her business. She never seemed to think anything about the war was her business (a lot of Austrians suffer from this), and she never faced the crimes the Nazis committed, the genocide that rid Austria of the many great minds who built and modernized the city she adored. In the summer of 2003, when I went to Vienna for a month to research a novel I never wrote, I saw a photograph of Herbert in the mountains around Salzburg, taken before the war. There are, as always, the pretty girls with bows in their hair. Herbert has his shirt off and a kerchief tied around his neck. They are sitting in picnic tranquillity beneath a

Nazi flag they have planted. The shot was taken from above, at a long distance, and below them a quiet green valley sprawls toward hills in the distance.

I inherited Herbert's military keepsakes – his medals, his decorations (all of which incorporated swastikas), his uniform buttons. I was the only one of his grandsons who showed real interest in my Austrian heritage, and it was Maria's decision to let me keep them. After my parents divorced and I moved with my mother from San Antonio to Conroe, just north of Houston, I used to march around the house wearing an amalgamation of these things and my father's US Navy aviator's jacket, hat, and officer's ribbons.

When the Russians invaded Vienna, all the young women went out of their way to make themselves ugly. The stories they heard of Russian infantry had everyone in a state of delirious terror. They were raping all the girls and women and killing everything else: babies, boys, and old men. Only old and hideous women, so it went, were safe. Maria changed the names of her boys to Petrovich and Nikolai. When the Russians came, the soldiers, she said, raped her every day, several times a day. This is something I learned very late – during a telephone conversation in 2003 – though I had heard about the changing of the names, and many other stories, from an early age. The soldiers liked the boys' names – perhaps they found the misuse of the patronymic for my uncle charming – and didn't kill them. Eventually she and the boys fled the city. She used to tell a magnificent story about running down a long road out of Vienna with many other women and children. She had Peter in one arm and my father in the other, and explosions followed them. I have no context outside the immediacy of that image. I have no idea what road they were on. I don't know if they were headed south or west. I see her, the boys, other people, trees, smoke. It's like a scene from a movie – what have I experienced that would lend it authenticity?

A lot of people, she said, gave up. The fear paralysed them. Some women begged others to take their children. A lot of these people were captured rather than killed, she said, but the Russians left a lot of dead on that road.

She found refuge on a farm. This farm emerged naturally in her memory but is incongruous to me, now: why did no one else go there? Why was it safe, if they were being chased? Why did the Russians continue to pursue the Viennese outside the city, since from the sound of it the Nazi army was nowhere to be found? Was it, possibly, that the farm is another memory entirely, that somehow got entwined with the road? Is it possible that I have it all wrong – that the road came during the first wave of invasion, and the farm came only after the Americans arrived?

I intended to ask such questions – not only about the road and farm but about everything, especially Herbert – during that conversation in 2003. I had just returned from Vienna, and my interest in that past had been reignited by the photographs I'd seen of Herbert, by speaking nothing but German for a month, by a book about Hitler's Vienna, by the city itself. But when she mentioned, almost as an aside, that like many young women she was raped by Russian soldiers, and when I asked her to repeat herself, she said, with a breeziness that made it seem unlikely she was exaggerating, *Yes, hundreds of soldiers, hundreds of times*, I was too embarrassed to continue the interview.

My cousin Fielding – Maria's grandson by a different grandfather – told me recently that Maria has a boyfriend in the nursing home, but the man thinks he is a teenager, and they hold hands and whisper to each other. When Fielding went to visit her, the man told him: I like your daughter very much. Then he tried to sell himself as a suitor. Maria believes she still runs errands for Fielding's parents. She does not know how long she's been at the home – her presumption is about a week, though it has been more than a year – and she talks with pride about the fact that she stays busy, and drives her car all around the city. The most considerate thing to do is agree with her; otherwise she becomes distraught.

My stepmother tells me the home takes its residents for day trips. They board a bus and drive outside the city, under the impression they are headed somewhere, and look out the windows at the countryside, which, to many, surely, exists in a state of ceaseless evaporation. A few hours later they return, having not left the capsule of the bus.

It is autumn in Dublin, chilly and dark. I am sleeping with socks on. My Vespa is barely alive in the mornings, and seems to recoil at the sight of me. I have to wear a hat in the house to avoid headaches. I am trying to save money by not turning on the heat, but Elísabet is walking around in winter coats asking if there are any more blankets for her bed. She has been here several weeks and will leave before Christmas – my first housemate since Chicago, ten years ago. She is an Icelandic playwright, novelist, and performance artist. I don't know what to make of her, but I like her. Very little she says makes any sense. She sleeps like a hibernating bear. She drinks a lot of milk. She went to an AA meeting in Malahide a few weeks ago, and now she is running the meetings. Everything that happens becomes one of her stories. A few days ago she lost her notebook, and now she is writing a novel in which a strange creature sets a character on a quest, but the creature does not know what the quest is, since it lost the notebook.

Elísabet – who is the kind of person who finds meaning in her dreams, in accidents, in the offhand comments of total strangers, and who believes tiny people live under rocks – is fascinated by Maria's history, and wonders if her stoicism comes from a monumental coldness. Though this is not the Maria I know, it is of course possible. It might explain her relationship to the truth of the past, which she no longer has to face. She has escaped the guilt of complicity. Nobody can talk of Austrian grandparents who fell in love during the war without millions of dead Jews bringing it all back into perspective. Her suffering, I must remind myself, is nothing to anybody but us. Herbert's death is nothing to anyone but us.

Often Elísabet and I discuss her as though she were dead. I have placed a black-and-white picture of Maria and Herbert on my dining-room table, and Elísabet says it gives the house a sense of mourning. Herbert is seated in a wicker rocking chair, in his officer's uniform – grey trousers and jacket, black collar, white epaulettes – with one leg stretched out and the other bent. He is holding his left hand in his right hand on his lap. The top of his head is dressed in a white bandage. Maria is standing behind the chair, leaning forward, with her arms around Herbert's chest. Her cheek is touching his head. She, too, holds her left hand in her right hand. Maria has high cheekbones and wide-set eyes. She has dark, shoulder-length hair that is pulled back from her face. They are smiling, but Herbert isn't looking at the camera – he looks as though he's just been told something mildly funny by a person standing to one side. The shadows behind them spill a long way, and there are no leaves on the little tree they are sitting under. I can't tell anything from it. I can't tell if they are happy or sad. The embrace seems formal and slightly posed. Surely he is leaving for the front again, and they are already married. She is probably pregnant, though she may not know it. The picture I have in the frame is not even a photograph. It is a granulated printout of a digital scan of the original, which was destroyed a few years ago by a flood in Texas.

Elísabet and I have spent hours interpreting the picture. She says Maria's cardigan reminds her of the bricks at Auschwitz. She wants this chapter to begin: *My grandmother's cardigan reminds me of the bricks at Auschwitz.* I fear that I am not suited to that kind of writing.

After the war, the story becomes more coherent. Maria got work at a US Air Force base outside Vienna. I can't recall what her job was, though she told me on a few occasions. One day she was invited to eat breakfast with some of the officers – she was still very beautiful – and she broke down and wept at the sight of bread and jam. When she told them she could not eat something so extravagant when her children were starving – my father was suffering from rickets – they began to send her home with baskets of food. It is the only episode she tells from her entire life that makes her wistful.

In 1947 she received a letter from an American officer she'd met when he'd worked at the base, Jim Baxter, asking her to come to Oklahoma and marry him. There was a picture of him in the letter. He mentioned his love for her, which had grown since they parted. He mentioned his job and stability. Her family convinced her there was nothing in Austria – no money or food, no men. She moved to Oklahoma and married Jim; shortly after that they relocated to Texas – the Alamo Heights district of San Antonio. Jim adopted my father and Peter, and they took his surname.

Jim and Maria had a child together, Jim Jr – Fielding's father. They divorced in the early 1980s: Jim, then in his sixties, left Maria for a 33-year-old. Though I called him *Opa* (as I called Maria *Oma*), and he raised my father, I have no memory of him. I must have been around him quite a bit as a child, but I never noticed.

Maria was unfazed by the divorce. She had never loved him, she explained. She was merely loyal and regretless. Many years later she would admit that her trepidation in emigrating came not just from leaving Austria – she *was* a patriot – but because she hardly even remembered Jim Baxter.

A few years after the divorce, Maria began working as a nurse for a woman with Alzheimer's outside the town of Boerne, about thirty miles north of San Antonio, where the Texas Hill Country begins. When the woman died, her husband, Bob Wallace, a rich attorney with a big white Cadillac and a big red Cadillac, proposed that, since they were old anyway, and he had some money, and would like to travel in Europe with a companion, they ought to get married. She agreed – the prospect of annual trips to Austria sold her. There was no ceremony I knew of, or if there was, no children were invited. Bob hated children. He could not tolerate irrationality. During meals he sat us around a humiliatingly small table, far away from the adults. Yet he had childlike fascinations and habits. He kept loaded guns all over his house and refused to move them, even though the idea that some marauder would be targeting his house was ludicrous. He was a ham radio operator. He was learning, at the age of eighty, computer programming, and obsessively played a golf game on his PC; he allowed me to play with him, and the fact that I always won was incomprehensible to him, and humorous. He seemed emotionless, and yet he used to cry at the sound of classical music. I interviewed him once for a high-school project, and realized he was the most interesting person I had ever known. The tape of that interview is lost, and I've forgotten everything he said, everything but this: once, when he was poor and starving, during the Depression, he had cleaned himself up, walked into a diner and ordered two large steaks. When it came time to pay the bill, Bob told the owner he had no money at all, but he'd work for his food. The man threatened to call the police, and Bob argued that he'd never get his money that way. He got a job as a dishwasher, then a cook. A few years later he was the lead attorney in Texas for FDR's Civilian Conservation Corps.

I sit here, at the dining-room table, beside the picture of Maria, waiting for this memory to spark others. Something comes back: I remember sitting in the room with him, checking the tape to make sure it was running. Flipping it when it stopped.

His house was situated at the top of a tall hill, and he owned the whole hill, down to little streams and thick woods that surrounded it, which was unused land for the most part. He had a salt lick and used to sprinkle dry kernels of corn all around his yard, and mobs of deer used to migrate through the space while we watched from the back patio. They would stop and eat everything, and we had to be absolutely quiet or they would spook and trample away. My father and Bob spent a lot of time chipping golf balls around. Bob argued with other men about politics and philosophy and religion, and whether he was right or not, he always won the arguments. Nobody could keep up, or wanted to. He was a devout atheist –

unlike my father, who was a private and disinterested atheist. He called black people niggers and did not understand why they wanted to be called anything else – and by anything else (this dates him rather severely) he meant *coloured*. When lots of grandchildren visited, the boys played war in the woods, and the girls did indoor things. Maria often wore a dirndl and baked. We had transplanted the Aryan dream to the Texas Hill Country.

I spent a lot of time at that house by myself. Because I cared the most about my Austrian heritage, I was the favoured grand-son. I slept in a big bed in one of the large guest bedrooms. In the daytime it was fine, but at night the ceiling filled with tiny scorpions that cast great vampiric shadows in the lamplight. I wrapped myself up to my neck in a blanket and slept like a plank of wood. I told Bob he had scorpions in his house and he looked at me very much like I expected him to.

At the age of eighty-five, Bob suddenly became sick: emphy-sema and a dozen other illnesses. His mind was still fierce – he remembered everything that ever happened; he wanted to get out and exert the influence of his mind on the world – but he could not control when he went to the bathroom, couldn't walk on his own, could barely breathe and depended on an oxygen mask. His condition transformed Maria from a wife to a nurse. One day he sent her out for groceries and took his army issue .44 and blew his brains out. She found his body, which she never described. He was the first person I ever personally knew who died. A few days later I telephoned her and asked how she was. I'm fine, she said, how are you?

A few days ago I was virtually alone on the Dart from my part of town to the city. After a few dry weeks, Dublin had finally come alive in the rain. No city in the world transforms in rain like Dublin. In the sunshine it is hard-edged and ugly and rank. In the rain it softens like a sponge, swelling, and all the open spaces narrow. The train passed out of the trees and suburbs and graffiti, where it rises over the houses slightly, above Clontarf, and the whole grey city was like a swamp floating in the bronze light of an overcast sunset, twinkling and shimmery building tops, rays of heavy rain slamming onto certain streets, this one and that one, and the bay, settled, chopless, paralysed. Above it, great blue-black clouds like Zeppelins rumbled hulkingly toward the city. It seemed like an invasion. An overweight woman with nice black hair, my age, sat a few seats ahead of me in a woolly black coat, reading a magazine. Another guy, handsome, in his twenties, on the telephone ahead of her, was talking to a girl. He was being very smooth. The train began to decelerate as we approached Connolly Station. The view of the bay was lost, and the high vantage, and so was the curious sense, which strikes from time to time, that I was not me but Herbert, suddenly alive after sixty-five years, but with no memory and no acquaintances. I stood and waited by the doors. The rain became so heavy, all at once, that the city disappeared completely.

I have a sense that somehow I must find a way to die in Vienna: I have never felt that I belonged anywhere else. Fielding came to Dublin from Texas a month ago, a few weeks after Elísabet arrived. He had been writing a seven-page philosophical essay for twelve months – the story of the possibility of a true self told in narrative – and needed some form of release to mark the end of it; otherwise he might go on revising forever. We have turned out to be radically different people, and I wonder if Herbert is responsible. Fielding is deeply optimistic about the future and doesn't drink much. He is unconcerned about specifics of his past, and perceives humanity as a fragmented tissue of souls that must look forward if it is to achieve a state of perfection. Like Elísabet, he looks for connections that help to piece together our understanding of ourselves and the world. His essay is tender and sorrowful. I told him it was an unconscious autobiography and he told me my essays were clumsy philosophies. When I asked if he thought often of Vienna, he said he hadn't much reason: Maria was his only link, and she was just a person – whereas for me she had, since the onset of her dementia, become a symbol of my lost and unrecoverable self.

Day by day, now violently, now effortlessly, I loosen my involvement in the world, my connections to people. Maria never succumbed to the temptation of regret; I live by the rule of it. Everything, to me, is out of reach; it has passed. Elísabet and Fielding search for illumination, a reconstituted paradise. I dream of a city that exists in perpetual nighttime.

After Bob's death, Maria moved into a small apartment in Alamo Heights, not half a dozen streets from her first house in Texas. She had a few more marriage offers but was not interested. Perhaps she had loved Bob, though she never said so. Or maybe she was bored of men. She walked two miles a day with a fat dog that couldn't keep up with her. She used to play a lot of bridge, and was extremely good, but by then her partners were either dead or too sick to get together. She found part-time work at a second-hand clothes shop, and, as she believes she still does, ran errands for Fielding's parents. She wanted to stay busy. She didn't need the money, since Bob had left her enough to go on comfortably for quite some time. But she was already becoming forgetful – small things – and wanted to stay active. She returned to Vienna a handful of times, twice with me: once to take me on my first trip there, at the age of fifteen, and again when I lived in Germany for a year, at twenty. We wrote letters (in German) when I was abroad – Germany, England, Ireland – and talked on the telephone when I was in America – Austin, Chicago, Baton Rouge. Signs of her mental deterioration were present when I still lived in the States: sometimes on the drive from her house to ours, she would get lost on roads she had driven a thousand times, and call us in a panic. Sometimes she telephoned my step-mother many times a day to ask the same question. These episodes made her angry, and soon there was almost no conversation she had that was not about how terrible it was to lose one's memory – which was no different than one's sanity – or some pill that would fix her. Nevertheless, she remained deeply unaware of her diminished independence, or refused to accept it – this was the woman who had run down a road with two sons in her arms, fleeing the Russian army. Once, on her way to visit me in Baton Rouge, when her connecting flight in Houston was cancelled by bad weather, she hitchhiked four hours in a car with a strange man rather than stay in a hotel.

Every night, for many years after Bob's death, she had dinner with a woman named Eve, who lived in a big ranch-style house a few streets away. Eve, a rich widow and constant Scotch drinker – old-school Texas ball-breaker, the kind of woman who is sophisticated and ladylike and smarter than all the men she knows and takes no shit – was Maria's oldest American friend. She was a lot like Bob in the end: outspoken and sharp, but an invalid. Maria ran all her errands (even though Eve could've paid a service), cooked her dinner, did chores around the house. Their friendship was deep, and as Maria's memory eroded, it became symbiotic. I hardly knew Eve, but on the few occasions I visited she acted as though I might be one of her own grandchildren – though she never had children. Perhaps Maria shared us with her. When Eve died, Maria's mind seemed to crash into the reality that the last person in the world who relied on her – who had some need for her beyond the purely emotional – was gone. She lost a great deal of acuity at this time and never fully recovered.

On the first of our two visits to Vienna, in July 1990, Maria and I arrived at the train station at around nine in the evening. We had taken the train from Frankfurt, a nine-hour journey I mostly slept through. Maria tried to wake me dozens of times to watch the scenery. I was too dozy to take note of much, and I missed, to Maria's supreme disappointment, the sight of the Danube through Passau.

We were met at the station by our immediate relatives, the Heusslers. They were standing on the platform in a kind of anticipation I hadn't expected, quiet, still, near disbelief, as though they suspected I might not be real. None of them had ever seen one of Maria's grandchildren, and it was decided, immediately, that I was – and Erika gasped when she said it – an exact duplicate of Herbert. Maria had taught me a few phrases – *Es freut mich sehr, dich kennenzulernen* and *Ich küss die Hand, gnädige Frau* – but even after two years of high-school German I found them difficult to remember and was too embarrassed to use them.

It was the first time I had been outside the US. It was also the first time I had been to a city, or rather, my first realization that places like San Antonio and Houston were not cities at all but vast and loose agglomerations of parking lots.

We went straight from the station to the Heusslers' apartment – Amalienstrasse 11, Ober St Veit – an address that was etched into my mind: everyone assumed I'd get split from the group and be utterly lost. Three generations of the family lived together in one building: Erika on the top floor with her husband Kurt; their son Dieter with his wife Heidi on the floor below them; and, in the basement, in a little room with only a bed, a small refrigerator full of smelly cheese, and a record player, Walter, my cousin. His brother, Michael, had long since moved out. I spent a lot of my nights in Vienna in that basement, chatting with Walter. Maria was concerned that he was a bad influence because she thought he was gay and a drug addict. He kissed his male friends fully on the mouth, worked part-time as a shop-window designer, and, well, acted generally gay. Of course, he *was* gay, and so was his brother Michael, who taught ballroom dancing.

That first night, we ate a dinner of bread, meats, and cheeses. I had expected the kind of meal Maria made for us – the over-abundant plates of goulash and Wiener schnitzel. I ate so much they had to bring out whole new platters. They watched in awe as I ate and ate. Maria told them, This is nothing. At home I make him ten pork chops. He never stops.

By day, Maria and I, sometimes with the Heusslers and sometimes on our own, took excursions to famous sights, museums, galleries, small cafés, and heurigers high up in the hills around the city. Maria needed no map. She hopped on and off streetcars and the U-Bahn with certainty and exuberance. We met a schoolmate of hers, and many friends of the family. She took me to laneways and street corners that had significance in her life, to the house where she grew up, the shelter where she took Nick and Peter to during bombing raids. Seventeen years later, I remember almost nothing of the conversations we had, but I try to clear my thoughts entirely, so that her voice might reappear. I remember only her happiness, not just for her but for me, because I had accepted wholly the fact that half of me was Viennese.

The second time we went, four years later, she would get lost quite easily and panic. She talked a lot about how she couldn't remember her German, or the names of her favourite places, or where they were. I became the guide. I was living as an exchange student in Würzburg, Germany, at the time, old enough to go to bars with Walter and Michael and smoke hash in cars on the way to raves. I spent hardly any time with her, just hungover lunches before the drinking began again. By then, however, she was glad of all that. It turned out she thought boys who behaved themselves were abominations.

Before we travelled to Vienna that second time, she had come to visit me in Würzburg. I showed her the city and the university. She stayed in a pension near my dorm, and there we discussed her life in earnest. She knew her memory was going. I introduced her to my friends, many of the beautiful girls who lived in my dorm. When I introduced her to the girl I was dating, she was polite but aloof. Later, she told me it was no good to have one girlfriend: I must have them all. It is in contemplating this remark, now, sitting at my dining-room table, beside the photograph, that I sense what kind of man Herbert may have been.

Elísabet tells me she can see Maria in our house, sitting beside me at the table, waiting patiently for her story to come to something. How I wish this were the case, that I had within me the capacity to do her life justice. Elísabet's mind creates: it is astounding to watch. Sometimes she will have a thought and start quietly dancing. She believes the world is always telling truths, and she listens. A mountain told her to write a play about her father. An American football game told her to finish a book. She is always going for coffees with people she meets on the Dart. She finds boring people inspiring. Since men are inherently dull, she turns them into obsessions. She could fall in love with a peanut. It is as though someone built a weird machine designed to debunk monotony. She is like a child playing hide-and-seek with her own thoughts. Once, I saw her outside the house and she began to clap and shouted from a long way off, Hey! We are in *Ireland*!

When I first arrived, I experienced such moments. They would arise for no reason, in unspecial settings, in the middle of daily routines. The feeling has no light or shape or colour, only, for a moment, a temperature. By the time you have named it, you have forgotten it. The imposition of a word is the act of forgetting. A man who wishes to transfer his experience to the page might as well try to throw a typewriter at the moon.

My life is the opposite of an adventure. In this I am like almost everybody, except I will not struggle in the grip of delusion. I will remain very still, its hold will relax, and I will slip out. Maria always wanted me to return to Vienna. It was she who inspired me to live in Germany for a year, where I met an Irish woman who would introduce me to the woman I would marry. Maybe one evening I'll arrive in Vienna unannounced. I will find a small flat just outside the Ring – something I can afford for a little while – with a view of nothing much. I will go grocery shopping and read books; with diminishing impact I will live out the resurrection of a dead history.

4
Health.
Success.
Children Every Year.
Die in Ireland.
(A Toast)

Just the other morning, the cold came back. It had struck the city for a week in October, but it left like a disinterested ghost. The sky was floating very low above the houses, and blue, and the streets had been licked by a little rain in the night. I stood on my terrace for half an hour, up early, drinking a few glasses of water. The Belfast train shot through a gap in the estate, which is still under construction; lit on the inside, bleared in its velocity, a whir of violet and grinding.

The first day of winter, not by date but in essence, the first day you realize you are not waiting, but *in it*: the sun slowly drained the blue off; the sky became the colour of whalebone. Or the colour I imagine whalebone to be: it reminded me of the sea – hulking, low, wet, and bodily. I went downstairs to leave for work. I unlocked my Vespa from the concrete column that holds up the front of my house. I bundled up: rain gear, scarf, headphones, helmet, gloves – summer gloves – still wet from the day before. The first flights of the day were descending over the estate from the east, in from the sea. When the clouds are especially low, the jets materialize above the coastline, which is less than a mile from me. The sound they make is like a little avalanche, or one that is huge but very far away. It is an elemental image of my twenties, a time when my life consisted of elemental images, when almost every year I moved to a new country: descending through cloud, as though gobbled up in the whale's mouth, the sudden disappearance of pure light, shot through the crystal of pure atmosphere, a minute of turbulent blindness, through the gut, then excrementally dropped into the weak-lit air above the city, moving, wet, matchbox: Vienna, Frankfurt, London, Dublin, Chicago, and the little cities I lived in between them.

The scooter woke up the sleepy street. A woman packing child accessories into her car stopped to glance in my direction. I gave a little wave and she responded with a smile.

Life on my Vespa is precarious. I have a problem with a ball bearing, or so I have been told – I have no idea. My front wheel wobbles at slow speeds, and badly on slick surfaces. I hold the handlebars like a bad tightrope walker holds a balancing stick, weaving between jammed lanes, trying to avoid wing mirrors.

It is almost December, and the city centre has been lit up for Christmas; the lights and decorations are strung from buildingtop to buildingtop, and in the dark evenings they reanimate the twinkling sense of childhood gaiety, except drunk and spending money: snowflakes on George's Street, bells and angels, *Nollaig Shona Dhuit* in lights, over and over, on Henry Street, and giant new chandeliers on Grafton Street. The journey from my door to the door of my office lasts thirty minutes, though I have, through the great denying power of the mind, convinced myself it takes twenty, so I am always late. It means nothing, since I take a coffee break immediately, and since, if I do any work at all before lunch, it is only to write my own things, and email Katie, a strange, erratic and lonely 24-year-old Welsh girl with an athletic body and tattoos. Only on Mondays, when we go to press, do I heave a little effort toward the paper.

When I am sent to daytime conferences, I tend to pay them short and angry visits. Afterwards, I take my Vespa all around the city, listening to loud music. Once I drove out to Sandycove Strand and sat on a bench with a book, bundled up tightly, and looked out to the sea, but I felt like an idiot. A few times I have parked at Dun Laoghaire pier, and thought of walking it, to stare in the direction of where I live across the grey width of the bay. But I am not that kind of person, as much as my old self wanted me to be. Now, I like to whiz around Stephen's Green and soak in the sight of good-looking women, and I like to drive around hardscrabble portions of the city, stop on footpaths and smoke cigarettes, observing people pushing buggies around without babies in them.

My weeknight dinners are always the same – a tuna sandwich with mustard on brown bread at the Centra on Parnell Street, thirty minutes before class begins. I have been eating the same sandwich every Monday through Thursday for months, and always order from the same woman, though she never gives any sign of recognizing me. I eat, standing, at one of two tall tables that are also rubbish bins, and people throw their trash away under my elbows. The television high in the corner is tuned to *Sky News*, which I watch inattentively, because there is no sound out of it.

Within and around the edges of the pattern of my working day, I foist nothing upon the accidental nature of the world. My observations stand without the imposition of plots or meaning:

Health. Success. Children Every Year. Die in Ireland. (A Toast)

I am not interested in fictions. I have used up all the characters in my head. They are all at the beach. They have walked off the pages of all my old stories and gone to Mexico. A lot of them swam out in the ocean and are dead. Those who remain hang around a bar and watch the sea all day. They move from job to job. The sun boils them. They fuck each other in dirty motel rooms. They go drinking and fall into gutters, where they lie unconscious for days, and in the rainy seasons, when the streets flood and the mud from the green mountain slops down like a fat brown tongue, their bodies float around like empty aluminium cans. This is the end of them, the Giudecca in the hell of the free self.

After class, the students and I head down to the Hop House on Parnell Street, a sadly decorated Korean sushi restaurant and sports bar with cheap pitchers of beer. It is full of young Korean dudes with freakishly beautiful girlfriends, and, worryingly, an increasing number of Dublin hipster types, the gig-goers in hats and T-shirts and beards and jittery on E or amphetamines.

The drive home is up the same streets I came down fifteen hours before, empty but for taxis. I run all the red lights. I come home and fall into the couch.

From out of this paralysed universe comes the concussive reality of women. These days I am up to my neck in luck.

I hate a surly and gloomy spirit that slides over the pleasures of life and seizes and feeds upon its misfortunes. [Montaigne]

I am annoyed that my essays serve the ladies only as a public article of furniture, an article for the parlour. This chapter will put me in the boudoir. [Montaigne]

I carry, through the static tableau of my everyday routine,

memories of bodies and the noises they make, the positions they prefer, the intricate texture of beauty – moles, bellybuttons, breastbones, fat and skinny nipples, wet cunts, irises, teeth, callused bottoms of feet, smudged make-up, freckles on noses, toenails and fingernails.

I like women who are so pale they can disappear in white bedsheets. Undressing them in my bedroom, they glow white in the street light. When we wake, they are the colour of cold mornings. I like them falsely demure – they blush at the mention of things they desire, and things they do.

My former housemate Elísabet – who is something of a sensation in her country, and only dates men half her age – writes very beautifully about sex because she is not afraid of what people will think. She says an orgasm is like a hand that reaches up inside her, grasps her by the spine, and shakes her like a rattle, an inch away from the death of one self and the rebirth of another. I have no capacity to write beautifully about sex. Often I am battling through the swamp of a dozen pints, the smoke of twenty cigarettes, and no real sleep for days. The exercise is nauseating, and I feel like the young Orwell working in a small, hot, Paris kitchen.

There is a blonde named Juliette who comes three or four times during one long act of fucking. She can come just from humping with clothes on, even giving head. She lectures in physics to undergraduates. She got her PhD for something that did not interest her, and now she is wandering disinterestedly through post-doc research, and resents academia. She has very bright brown eyes and does not hold her drink.

Olivia, a junior doctor, has a problem with falling when she gets drunk, and likes tequila. She gives head with the enthusiasm you only find in good Catholics, and she, who usually doesn't sleep with men she likes for months, lies around in the mornings wondering what has happened to her morals. She is nearly thirty but could pass for nineteen. This creates a funny incongruity – she is always saying things that seem too wise for her years. Because she works very hard in a competitive field that prizes success at the expense of others, she is also slightly mean-spirited. She sees right through romance and does not trust men. She has straight brown hair that she is proud of, and a wide mouth. She is enormously pretty but looks uncannily like a cousin of mine, which makes me feel uncomfortable. She comes with an almost unnoticeable shiver.

Allison, who is in public relations, has long brown hair that she can wear in a hundred different styles, and large eyes – so large and sad they are the first thing you notice – in a face that narrows sharply toward her mouth. She writes short stories on the weekends. They are all about people who can't talk to each other. When she kisses, she throws her head back in what I would call premature ecstasy, with her eyes open, and moans. She is very funny and quiet until she gets three or four pints inside her, and then she starts marching down the middle of busy streets telling men to fuck off. When she is underneath me she is always squirming away – it is like some *National Geographic* article in which the female is only subdued if the male can penetrate her. She tells me I am hurting her in a weak and crying voice but if I stop or slow down she looks at me as though I've ruined the moment.

Then Evelyn. Evelyn is the type of woman who has read all of Proust, whom I have only read one book of, but who also loves television shows about deformities and surgeries, which she can watch while eating dinner – while I have to look away and make loud noises. I am in love with her, but she has as little interest in hearing it as I have in saying it. Evelyn is afraid of having sex in bright light, and is always covering her naked body. She has a beautifully shaped and scentless cunt. It is perfectly symmetrical and inconspicuous. It is small but gets extremely wet. I crawl between her legs and admire her. I begin to lick her slowly and heavily, then quicken. I have my hands on her ass, lifting her to me like a giant delicious plate of food. When she is breathing quickly and moving around a little, I slip my middle and index fingers inside her. She begins to moan and almost writhe. A few minutes later I move both fingers into her ass. This is one way she comes. I press it past the quivering muscle, there is a sensation of a pop, then empty heat. Then slowly, all the way, I push inside her. And now I am licking her as fast and as lightly as I can, and sucking her clitoris. Her orgasms are like quiet emergencies – she whispers that it's on the way, repeats herself three or four times, convulses for a few moments, moaning Oh God or something like it, then grabs and holds herself with all her fingers pressed flat and hard on her cunt. And then I climb up her long body and if my dick has gone flat it goes hard the moment it's in contact with her. She is ten times more beautiful being fucked than doing anything else, because it is only being fucked that you may witness all of her. She is too inscrutable to gauge at any other time. This is a woman who blushes when she is asked to speak in public but likes to watch herself giving head in mirrors. She has conveniently mounted a narrow mirror into the wall beside her bed, and we often fuck sideways so both of us can watch. Sometimes when I am on top of her, her head slips over the edge and she watches herself upside down. She likes to be fucked with great energy, which she absorbs in near silence. When there is no mirror, just us, and I am on top of her, she keeps her eyes half-closed for the most part, staring at nothing. I gaze at her face. Slowly she lifts her eyes and looks at me, and does not look away. After I have come inside her and rolled exhaustedly off, we lie close to each other for a few minutes without speaking, and then she asks how long before we go again.

A few others have come and gone. A very small girl – just barely five foot – who is sweet and emotionally fragile came only when I fucked her from behind and immobilized all her limbs. A receptionist, aged thirty-nine, could not come at all – never once in her life, she said. A few came from intercourse, but only when they were on top and motoring at full speed. One came only when I made her talk about fucking other women – she is bisexual, only twenty-three. One night we met a girlfriend of hers at a bar. We got drunk and walked around the city looking for a taxi. When we found shadows or stretches of emptiness I would kiss one of them, or both of them, and they might kiss each other while I put my hand down the front of one's jeans. We got a taxi and pretended to be normal for twenty minutes, talking about this and that. We went to my friend's place – straight to her bedroom, which was filthy and smelled of mildew – and they both knelt down in front of me and took turns sucking my dick. Periodically they licked each other's mouths. Then I put them on the bed. I fucked one from behind while she kissed the other. Then I fucked the other on her back while the first straddled her face. The first became faint and lay to one side, but kept one leg under the other's head, so that I could watch the other lick the first's clit while I

53

worked two fingers in and out of her cunt. We all came together, or pretended to.

This is a very different December from the last, most of which I spent shopping and at dinner parties where the hosts and guests tried to outdo each other with toasts and clean, large houses. I have probably tripled in biological age since then. I get winded walking up one flight of stairs. I've sprouted a few grey hairs at my temples. My deterioration gives me a sense of great freedom. My thoughts go unencumbered now. I approach a state of equilibrial disdain, disdain without heat. Wherever I see crowds, I avoid them. If I offend, it is not because I have sought to. If I please, it is an accident.

I spent a whole decade cultivating rage. I laboured to disappoint. I infected the people I knew with bitterness. I pulled them in close and betrayed them. I felt no remorse, just pity. I left the tiny battlefields of my relationships scorched and full of smoking corpses. I walked over the bodies without examination.

I like to call my Vespa midnight blue, but in truth it is dangerously close to purple. Not long ago, on my way to Evelyn's apartment in Leopardstown, I hit a large pothole in Donnybrook. I saw it too late, driving only a few feet behind a car at high speed, in the rain. I braced and slammed into it; to brake fully in wet weather on a Vespa is suicide. I think I said Oh SHIT. There was a loud crash and the handlebars popped out of my grip for a moment. My feet came off the little platform. I was disconnected from the bike for only half a second, but I was pretty certain I was dead. The hole was only a few inches deep but Vespas aren't very rugged. Primarily they are to be sat on while smoking cigarettes in Italy, talking to pretty girls. The hit sent a jolt right into my neck. For a few days I couldn't turn my head sideways, or lift it.

The first time Katie saw my scooter, she laughed. She said, in the most wonderful accent imaginable, Oh dear, and put her hand to her mouth. But your helmet? she said. It's for a real motorcycle.

Last week, Katie and I went ice-skating at the RDS for her birthday. A Canadian friend of hers, Patricia, came along. Patricia is a short girl with sturdy legs and a voice like shattered glass being rubbed into your eyes; but she has pretty brown hair, light freckles, and a nose so tiny that you feel you must touch it. Katie has phases in which she surrounds herself with as many people as possible, plays six or seven instruments at small sessions with friends, and goes after men with the gargantuan clumsiness of an elephant. But when she is feeling low she withdraws from crowds, assumes she will never be a good musician, and swears off romance forever. When she is happy she is like a large soap bubble, or thousands of them, blowing down a sunny street. When she is sad she is very pretty. That night she was feeling sorry for herself. She had made a point to invite nobody along to the ice-skating party, so Patricia and I had invited ourselves.

I had been ice-skating only once before, at the age of sixteen, so seventeen years later I was just trying to move around the rink without falling and shattering my wrists. The rink was small and almost square, so that as soon as you came out of a corner you were heading into the next. I took long rests every few minutes, stretching the cramps out of the muscles in my shins, and watched the girls race around the ice. Katie was pretty good. She was trying to learn the hop. Patricia skated with the effortless finesse and astronomical speed I had expected from a Canadian. There were a bunch of teenage boys there who were purposely crashing at full speed into the walls. One grabbed my shirt trying to regain his balance and, on purpose, I elbowed him in the face. Patricia, however, slipped gracefully through them. They tried to keep up but could not. She skated backward, taking photographs of Katie and me, faster than the boys could go forward. Now and again I'd mimic her style and almost fall over. My arms would spin and I'd go back and forth like a pendulum. She stayed low and smooth and instinctually aware of her surroundings. By the end of the night I'd learned how to take corners by crossing my legs, but that was it. Katie learned to hop and kept doing that. She was unaware, probably, that her large breasts were bouncing around in her tight black top, and that nearly all the boys and men, including me, were helplessly transfixed by them.

I am always hoping that one night she will give in to curiosity and fuck me. But women don't seem to fuck men out of curiosity, at least not friends.

Afterwards, we went to Mary Mac's and had cheeseburgers and cake – a cake that Patricia made at the table in the pub with ingredients she pulled out of a plastic bag. It was Monday, and the place was nearly empty. Mary Mac's had been a regular spot for me the year before, great for all-evening Friday drinks in summer. The girls ate the cake before the cheeseburgers. They nearly finished it. I had to slice a tiny piece and move it far away from them, and they even tried to eat that. When the food was finished, Patricia took a phone call from her boyfriend and disappeared for an hour. Katie and I sat together drinking. She mentioned, for the hundredth time, that she would leave Ireland soon but that she would never return to Wales. She wanted to live in a small village by the sea and play music. Her job was no good, but she needed the money for travel. She sighed, and then she snapped out of it. Underneath the table, I let my feet touch her feet. She didn't notice.

5
Glitter Gulch

I had to spend Christmas in Texas. It was out of my hands. My father had demanded, in the way he has of demanding, that I come home: he knew a thing or two about collapsed marriages. I left my house in the hands of Helen, a former student who owned a thousand books without covers (she worked in a bookstore), and who liked to dance on my dining-room table in the middle of the night; sometimes I watched from a chair, drinking whatever was left in the house.

I got home at four in the morning on the 21st, the day I was to fly out, and, having no clean clothes, threw some dirty boxers and socks and a pair of flip-flops into a large suitcase – I would buy clothing in Texas. After a long shower I went up to my little terrace and paced around in the streetlit dark. My taxi wouldn't be long, and I needed to stay awake. Since my heart probably couldn't take the strain of coffee, I decided to expose myself to the cold for half an hour. I had survived a month-long binge, and I couldn't trust myself to open my eyes if I closed them.

That night, I'd been drinking with John, another former student, at the Lord Edward, an uncomfortably lit and foul-smelling box near Christchurch, full of very calm old people. We'd ended up there after drifting from one unsatisfactory spot to the next. It was the Thursday before the city broke up, so everywhere was jammed – the bars, the footpaths, restaurants, shops. The following night would be worse, but I'd be five thousand miles away.

John is a big guy, handsome, at six foot two an inch taller than me, not fat but large-bellied. He always wears T-shirts and big jackets, never combs his hair, and shaves once a month. He was finishing a thesis for a master's in computer programming – or obsessing over its lack of progress. It had become – this tiny document – the most wretched and debilitating task in his life, and he could not talk about it without slipping into nonsensical rambling. He was the most talented writer I'd come across in a year of teaching, but it hadn't come together for him, and now, I knew, he was going to quit. His decision to commit murder on his talent was something I remorsefully admired – I had played a decisive role in John's dis-illusionment. I had passed on too freely my loathing for the propriety of *being a writer*, tried to help him find the pure and fearless voice of total disenchantment. During one of our conversations I said that a man who can write ought to commit an act of violence against literature or abandon it entirely. John had written three or four stories in his whole life.

We'd been at the Lord Edward for an hour when Olivia arrived. She had sent me a few texts in response to my invitation, aloofly intimating she might pop along, at some time, if she got bored of what she was doing, and wasn't too tired to go home, but she'd see. John and I were outside, smoking. We saw her only when she stopped in front of us. She walks so softly, arms always crossed, shoulders never rising or falling, that she seems to stand still. She wore heels – she wears heels to run across the street for bagels on Saturday mornings – and dark blue jeans.

Hey, I said.

Hey, she said, as though I had introduced myself at a nightclub, and she was not interested.

The three of us sat at the bar, and John and Olivia did most of the talking. I was wiped out, drunk, and had nothing clever to say – I just wanted to lie Olivia in front of me on the bar and go down on her, with everybody watching, her legs buckled over my shoulders, her arms knocking down glasses. Once I tried to speak and mispronounced *music*. They asked me to repeat myself, and I made the same mistake: *moosic, moosic*. I went for cigarettes to keep from drinking, but smoking just made me worse. Parts of me grew very heavy, such as my tongue, my brain, my eyelids, and my lungs. Olivia asked John if he was a writer, and his answer was to groan and say he'd done my classes. How's it going, she asked him. Not well to be absolutely fucking honest with you, he said.

Olivia went to the toilet at one point and John said, Fuck me, horse, she's good-looking.

It was the truth, and I knew she had men falling at her feet. But she didn't trust men. Once, while lying in bed after sex, I put my arms around her and she said, That's not necessary.

John left at ten, and Olivia and I decided to go to Wexford Street. The taxi took a long time, in heavy traffic, going up George's Street. Every laneway seemed to be occupied by a thousand bodies. The street between Hogan's and the Market Bar was impassable with people smoking. Two girls screamed insults at each other outside the Capital Bar. I was happy to be in this city, but not of it. If it had hit a wall then, it would have smashed entirely to chalk and glass and blood. I tried to hold Olivia's hand. She asked, What are you doing?

We went to Solas, which was the only place that didn't have a cover charge and wasn't impossibly packed. I'd drunk myself a little sober – this always strikes me as uncanny – so I was chatty again. We stood by the bar and I watched her in the mirror. Barbarically I tried to kiss her. I had my hands up the back of her shirt, and she wiggled away now and then. Another couple kissed beside us. Don't you see how disgusting that is? she asked, but after another vodka my hands were in her back pockets, and she was giving in. I lifted her onto her tiptoes and I kissed her open-mouthed and roughly, and she put her hand on the back of my head. The bar didn't notice. People ordered drinks beside us. When somebody knocked into her, she dropped out of my arms abruptly. She looked at me as though she might slap me and said: You can come home with me, but no sex.

No sex?

I can't.

Out of action?

Out of action.

I thought I'd say, I'll fuck you anyway. It was the truth. I like the bloody aftermath. But I caught myself.

I want to go back with you, I said.

It's probably pointless.

We went out to the street. It must have been around midnight, and I felt as though I might fall asleep standing up. There were free taxis everywhere, which saddened me a little, since I had hoped to kiss outdoors for a few minutes, and soak up the last bit of atmosphere – there would be none of it in Texas.

In her flat I wanted to make myself something greasy to eat, but her fridge and all her cupboards were empty, as usual. Every week she planned a big food shop, and every week something got in the way. I poured myself a glass of tap water. She sat on her couch, curled up in one corner. I sat on the other side and we listened to music on the radio. I yawned and checked the time on my phone.

What's wrong with you? she asked.

Huh?

You're usually on top of me by now.

But you sat so far away.

I *always* do.

I pulled her on top of me and looked at her for a while. She has big eyes and dark eyelashes. When I started trying to undress her, she crawled between my legs and blew me to the background noise of house or trance or industrial – I simply don't know what these terms mean, I only pretend to – and I pulled her hair back to watch my dick screw in and out of her mouth. I became the whole city, and I turned to chalk and glass and blood. Olivia was getting tired and out of breath. Little droplets of saliva and ejaculate, from many near orgasms, leaked out of her lips. When she stopped to catch her breath, I jerked myself off to come. She watched patiently, breathing. But I couldn't. I was too tired. I told her to put a towel down and we'd fuck.

Disgusting, she said.

Finally we lay down on the couch and kissed. I closed my eyes and opened them.

You're awake, she said.

What time is it?

Just past three.

I fell asleep?

While kissing me.

She was in the same spot, lying beside me with her left arm bent helplessly between us. The radio was still playing, but it wasn't loud anymore; it was something like jazz and very bad.

Sorry, I said.

It was romantic, she said. The snoring.

On the way home, in the taxi, I texted to say that I'd miss her, and would bring her back a souvenir.

You're a girl, she texted back.

And I felt that I was surely in love with her, or in love with a life in which she existed.

Hartsfield International, Atlanta (I)

I had a five-hour layover in Atlanta. My departure gate hadn't been assigned, so I walked aimlessly for a while. I found some underground tunnels that linked the terminals at their ends – normally one takes the main shuttle link that runs right down the centre like a spine. I stood on the slow conveyors in these half-mile-long tunnels, all by myself. There was no music.

When, after an hour of this, I saw that my flight still had no gate, I stopped in the smoking room – there are two in each terminal – asked an ugly woman beside me for a light, and chain-smoked three or four cigarettes so I wouldn't have to bother anyone else: the black dude checking his texts, the cute girl with a tattoo on her neck, the obese man in a white beard wearing an

NFL jersey, breathing as though he were about to dive underwater. The room was not ventilated well, there were few seats, and the ashtrays, which were deep, did not extinguish the cigarettes; they made a bonfire of them.

One man, on the phone, told his wife, Honey, I'm not smoking, *I'm in an airport*. Veterans and soldiers chummed up. A large bearded man, mid-forties, in a baseball cap and T-shirt with some writing on it, told a soldier, a short Latino with dimples in his fat cheeks, that running every morning in combat boots had busted his knees. He'd still be fighting, if they'd let him, if he had any cartilage left, and I knew it was the truth. Another old guy leaned in to the discussion; raspily he talked about his training, and the miles he ran uphill, and thanked the young Latino for defending his country.

I rejoined the non-smoking flow of the airport. I had three hours, and, sober, in the bright lights, the world's busiest airport, the Christmas muzak, news-stands, CNN at every gate, I had the rats. It was almost midnight in Dublin, and the poison of forty straight nights – a true but accidental number – was starting to flood from my armpits, crotch and forehead. I'd withdrawn completely from my job, producing a drip of news and analysis so trivial that I could not remember what I did from hour to hour. Outside of work, I re-energized. I'd been teaching four nights a week all autumn, and in December my classes had ended, meaning I had money and time. It had been hectic and drunken and sleepless.

Moving through the terminals, observing the state of permanent transit, of people checking email on their phones, going over presentations on their laptops, I felt as though I'd been thrown from my city like a man thrown from his car in a violent crash. My body was beginning to tremble. This was sobriety, sobriety before the big sweaty slumber. I was beginning to hallucinate in the lights.

By the time I'd got to Terminal C my gate had been posted, and I found a bar near by. There was one empty spot. I put my bag down and took out a book. There were two gigantic black women bartending. The really fat one said, Whachoo want, baby?

A beer, please, I said.

She stood behind the row of taps and opened her eyes widely. You got to be more specific, baby, she said. The name on her tag was Latisha.

I didn't recognize the brand – some microbrew, with pale, amber and winter ale versions. I'd forgotten that nobody in America just drank beer anymore.

The pale, I said. Is it good?

Oh baby, it's good. They're all good.

The other woman shouted, You get a shot for free, baby!

For free?

Free shot with any pint, the first said.

I looked down the bar, and everybody had shots. Okay, I said. Jack.

The other woman shouted, Howboutsometequilababy?

A man a few spots down shouted, Fucking tequila, baby!

The other woman said, All right, baby!

The man smashed a wadded-up five-dollar bill on the bar with the palm of his hand and said, Fucking tequila! Shit yeah, baby!

Everyone nodded.

Okay, I said, tequila, baby.

Premium for an extra two dollars, baby.

Fuck that shit, yelled a guy at the far end of the bar.

Yeah, I said, just the well.

You sure?

I'm sure.

The really fat woman said, Okay, ID, baby.

The guy next to me said, Teesha, how fucking old does a guy have to be to not get carded?

I looked at him. Teesha looked at him. Sorry, dude, he said.

I knew my US passport would be easiest, but some unhappy need to defy the whole setting, to resist re-identification, urged me toward the Irish passport.

IREland! Teesha shouted, and she showed it to the other woman, who did not look but exclaimed, IREland!

I had no doubt these women saw passports from all over the world every day, but they knew what sold chemistry.

Motherfuckers in Ireland start drinking at birth, the guy next to me said. His name was Jake and he was from California, but he lived in San José, Costa Rica, where he and his brother ran a property business. He was shaggy, in a T-shirt and flip-flops.

Welcome to America, he said.

San Antonio

It was sunny and warm on my first morning in Texas, and I sat beside my father's small pool for an hour or two in the late morning reading the sports section of the *San Antonio Express-News*, the worst ostensibly serious newspaper on earth, and a book called *Hatchet Jobs*, which I had found in some old boxes in the closet of my bedroom – boxes I'd always meant to ship to Ireland. My father had told me he had a surprise for me, and suggested I make no plans for the 24th, 25th or 26th. I knew what it was, of course – my father's annual Christmas pilgrimage to the Holy Land of his unorthodox existence, the Horseshoe Casino in downtown Las Vegas. I had been looking forward to a little cigarette-less sobriety in Texas, just to give my body a break, but, having skipped breakfast as usual – a habit my father passed on to me, perhaps – I was drinking Miller Lites and smoking my stepmother's Camel 100s.

My father's house is a modest three-bed bungalow. It is very spare, neither clean nor dirty. My father, when he's not working, watches a lot of golf and B-movies – he likes zombies – while drinking Miller Lites. He also plays card games on the computer, and my stepmother, Barbara, is always online or else drinking at Turtle Creek Tavern, a comfortable and windowless dive bar ten minutes away that opens at seven a.m. The Christmas tree in the living room looks absurd, but is earnest. At any moment, there are several abandoned cigarettes smouldering in ashtrays in various rooms. There is rarely any conversation, except about their cats – three of them, and one is gigantic and violent. There is a cool lifelessness about the place, and their lives have an unexaggerated harmony that I find comforting. I move, whenever I am home, from room to room without purpose. I look out windows for minutes at a time. I examine my father's exotic succulents. I walk out back and throw a football to myself.

It was not even sixty degrees, but I was sitting at the pool's edge, in jeans but barefoot, and without a shirt, sunbathing. My father was on the other side of the house, watering the driveway.

It had been years since I last read *Hatchet Jobs*, a collection of caustic book reviews that had, I believed, unearthed and chopped up the roots of American literary pretence. I had just given up trying to sell my first novel, and the book reassured me that the publishing world was founded on the corrupt and flawed belief that the hacks and imitators I despised, and whose status I coveted, were the most serious writers in the country. They had been exposed. It felt like vindication. If I could not succeed, I could at least hold everything outside my imagination in contempt. I come back to the memory of my pettiness as to the grave of a tyrannical father – you are glad he is dead, but you wish you were the one who killed him.

After a while it was time to go shopping. My socks and boxers had been washed and dried, but I had no shirts except for a few yellow-armpit V-neck tees, and only one pair of jeans, which I'd been wearing since Dublin. I showered. The water in San Antonio is so dry that it barely seems to touch you. I didn't have any toiletries, so I sprayed some old cologne, something from my high-school days, which hadn't stirred in many years, on my armpits and chewed some gum by way of brushing my teeth. I put on my cowboy boots – the one great and unique thing about Texas being that nobody looks at cowboy boots strangely. By the time I was ready to leave, my father was standing in the back yard drinking a Miller Lite in his dressing gown, smoking one of his many lit cigarettes, his legs planted in gigantic brown fuzzy slippers. He was watering the pool.

I went outside to tell him I was going, and he slipped me some money. He is like a Mafia Godfather sometimes: who carries cash around in his dressing gown? He is a private man, and always walking away from you, always wrapping up conversations you're trying to continue. He searches for empty rooms. He communes with crossword puzzles, which he finishes by memory, not pencils, and the *Wall Street Journal*. I don't know whether it's a lack of interest in his own intelligence or a repudiation of it, but I sense that everything in life depressed him except for his withdrawal from it.

He was, my mother tells me, a dedicated and obsessive intellectual in college, and bound for great things in scientific research. He used to work for days in labs without sleep, growing beards and not washing, and his mother and my mother brought him food and refused to leave until they'd watched him eat. I try to link that old self to the one I know, but they are totally incompatible. He was also a pool hustler – it was how he paid rent some months – and this is slightly closer to the man I know, whose affinities and habits are always denigrations of ordinary values. He chose to leave research for medicine in order to avoid Vietnam. His brother Pete was already fighting there – he flew helicopters – and wrote letters home telling my father to move to Mexico if they drafted him.

My father's house is on the north side of San Antonio, about fifteen minutes' drive, on the interstate, from the first jagged burps of the Texas Hill Country – one of the landscapes my first novel inhabited. I do not write to make up stories, or invent characters, or to capture something of the age, or speak to it. I write in order to annihilate the mystery and magnitude of places in my memory, to exorcize their possession of me. Driving through the landscape, past the shopping supercomplexes by the highway, none of which existed in my childhood – the city now stretches inconceivably outward, repetitively, serving no purpose beyond enlarging the dominion of convenience – I felt a grey and painless repulsion. It had nothing to do with unfamiliarity. It would be alien with or without the sprawl. I can never hope to experience it. I have destroyed it.

After shopping, I drove the old roads – stringy, narrow, roller-coaster – that my best friend and I used to race around: Old Babcock Road, Cielo Vista, Boerne Stage Road. We had spectacular races, squealing corners, risking empty outside lanes with no visibility, daring overtakes through soft shoulders, burying each other in dust. I was timid in everything else: this fearlessness is a mystery. Back now, driving my father's four-cylinder, hybrid Toyota, I took the roads slowly. I was out of practice anyway. Those back roads are still largely undeveloped and unchanged. I had driven them a thousand times during the period of my life in which every thought was a heart-pulverizing epiphany, but I felt nothing, not even the warm vacuity that fills the shells of old epiphanies. I was there for the first time, with that amnesiac pain of knowing it ought to mean something. I stopped for some barbecue in Leon Springs, a place with outdoor benches. Sometimes you are lucky and get bikers with handlebar moustaches, but mostly it's retirees and fat grandchildren. I wasn't hungry, but I always go there for a few strips of brisket smothered in barbecue sauce. I took the long way home, through my first girlfriend's old neighbourhood, past some of the houses my family used to live in. There was no effect. I returned to find my father standing curiously still beside his large grill, drinking beer. I was starting to come down with something, a chest cold, so we got takeout rather than cook, and watched a few bad movies. He drank himself peacefully to sleep on the couch. A few hours later, I did the same.

Las Vegas

We boarded the plane mid-morning Christmas Eve, and I could already feel my heart tightening. My father had a dozen free-drink coupons and told the stewardess, Keep 'em coming. Then he winked at her. She said, You got it, baby. She did not know that we actually meant it, however, and by the fifth or sixth order, she said, surely lying, You drank it all, there's no more.

My cold had worsened: earache, coughing, sore throat and head. I couldn't get comfortable. My father had started me on Cipro – he has a tendency to overmedicate – and I knocked the beer back in gulps, because sipping was too painful.

It was warm and sunny in Vegas, but the weather in Vegas is irrelevant. We took the interstate downtown – the Strip is for Disneyland gamblers and Gatsbys, and though I admit the cocktail waitresses are worth the high table minimums, splendour doesn't suit me; and it doesn't suit my father. We prefer dereliction. The Horseshoe is the kind of place that, if you are not ready for the stink, the chipped paint, the ugly waitresses, the nicotine smog from bad ventilation, the rancid bathrooms, and the super-elderly, will sadden you back to the airport. But if this is what you have come for, then you are in paradise. We arrived mid-afternoon. Barbara had checked me in already, so I dropped my bag off, reapplied some deodorant, and was at the bar in less than ten minutes.

I ordered a beer and a guy next to me struck up a conversation. I told him I live in Ireland. Well, fuck, he said, *Ire*land. And then the bartender said he'd like to go to Ireland with his family and started calling me *Irish*. The whole place smelled like morning

71

bar mist – the scent that is half mildew and half stale beer, which ripens in the light of day.

My father goes about his gambling ritualistically: he plays his four or five favourite slots for a few hours, warming up, before two long sessions at craps interrupted by dinner, then a long warm-down at a few progressive slots and finally Bobby's bar for a nightcap. Barbara plays video poker and slots, never tables, and she is always lucky. It is as though the gods sprinkle gold dust on her fingers. The next day, for instance, she would take over my poker machine at the bar so I could play roulette, and the first hand she got was a royal flush worth a grand. I am not lucky, and gamble like a cowardly scavenger. I sit at the front bar, which used to be Po's bar – Po was a tiny Vietnamese man who knew the injury status of every Division 1 football quarterback in America – anxiously pacing the room with my eyes. I try to be cool, because I know that tables and machines sense fear. That day I played twenty-five-cent video poker for free drinks, building a mountain of snot-soaked tissues and checking over my shoulder. After three or four beers I became drunk again, and I became invisible: for lack of interest the tables had looked away. I stood, cashed out, and felt for my wallet. Barbara, a hundred bucks up beside me, like it was nothing, said, Good luck!

I found my spot: an empty roulette table. I assumed she was lonely and unhappy, and would give herself freely. In hindsight I should have picked a full one, one already giving it up. I sat down and got a hundred dollars' worth of chips. The dealer, a tall man with a giant salt-and-pepper moustache, said, Which colour would you like? I hadn't expected the question, and I was stumped. Which was the luckiest colour? I saw myself at the edge of a great crashing whirlpool and rowed on in like an idiot.

Orange, I said. Ten minutes later I had nothing, not a single chip. I hadn't hit one number. The dealer said, Better luck next time. Humbled but alive with defeat, I went back to Po's bar and sat beside Barbara, who was up another fifty. How'd you do? she asked. Not good, I said. And the whole process started over again.

A man beside us was telling dirty jokes. No one of common decency joined the bar. Everybody was a jack of some unhappiness, some dispossession. There were some thugged-out black dudes who were trying to order drinks with loud *Yo*s and throwing large-denomination chips at the bar. Downtown, for a short time a decade before, had become a hot spot for the B-list hip-hop crowd – outside of rodeo week they had free rein there, and could act like kings – but there was no point flashing power and beauty around people who were trying to crawl back down the social ladder, or were entirely off it. All hope and prosperity flowed toward the Strip. People sometimes come downtown to sightsee the old Vegas, and they look upon it with disbelieving interest – why would someone pick this dump with the Bellagio only twenty minutes away?

We had had a plan to get prime rib and lobster at the top-floor restaurant, but Barbara wasn't hungry – she had not slept the previous night – and my father and I agreed that the prime rib in the downstairs diner was the same as you got on the top floor, at one-fifth the price, so we ate there.

I was down about three hundred dollars by the time midnight rolled around, Christmas officially, but my nose had stopped running and I felt fine. I had lost all that money at roulette. I found my father and Barbara at about half past twelve standing at Bobby's bar, talking to Bobby, a diminutive and ebullient Italian man who'd been there almost fifteen years. The barback – I've forgotten his name – looked as out of place as he could've been beside Bobby, recalcitrant and disturbed. Tall and hunched, he never smiled and spoke only to curse at small tips. Barbara said, Your dad almost got in a fight.

My father smoked his cigarette and grunted with indifference, saying: Fucking asshole.

He, my father, had been sitting beside Barbara at Bobby's bar, though Bobby hadn't been there, when a guy on the other side of him said, Hey, do you have to blow that smoke in my fucking face?

My father, who might have apologized if the guy had asked politely, said: Move to the non-smoking bar, you fucking asshole.

I had come too late to see what this guy looked like, but Barbara said he was huge and my father said he was fat. Either way, my father was too old to get into fights, and he had a cage surgically installed in his neck because his spinal cord, from arthritis, had started to fuse together. The guy continued to mutter insults until Bobby arrived and Barbara told him the whole story. Bobby told the guy and his friend, You just fucked with my best customers, get the hell out and don't come back. They refused, and the barback said to Bobby, I'll throw their asses out. Eventually they left, calling back to the whole scene, Downtown trash! My father's parting gesture was to give him the finger and shout, Goodbye!

I would've kicked his motherfucking ass, said my father, though he was already yawning and checking his watch. Not long after, he announced his departure. He wagged his finger at me: Don't stay up too late, we're starting early tomorrow – breakfast at eight.

Barbara and I chatted for a while at the bar, with Bobby intermittently joining us. There was no discernible evidence that Christmas had arrived, except that the casino was almost empty – nothing but Asians and the really really down-on-their-luck, the guys playing roulette and blackjack with drawn grey faces, rubbing their eyes heavily with the balls of their palms after big losses, or pulling their baseball caps very low.

Barbara said she was going to hit the sack as well. Your luck getting any better? she asked.

Worse, I said.

She grimaced. What are you playing?

Mostly roulette.

Maybe you should play some craps.

I think I'm done gambling for the night.

She started digging in her purse and I told her not to bother. I'll just lose it, I said.

That's the point, she said. She handed me three hundred dollars – all crisp notes, fresh from the endless wellspring of her unbelievable luck.

After she left I sat at the bar by myself wondering what I ought to do with what seemed to me a half-divine offering, a hand right out of the clouds – save it for the next day, try my luck again, or not gamble it at all, just take it back to Dublin, since outside of this surprise excursion I was a hundred kinds of broke. In a few months I'd be on an all-potato diet. I rolled this question around my head for a long time – maybe five minutes – before I decided to get up and walk around the casino and see what might happen. Maybe there'd be some girl to talk to, I considered, before discarding the idea. No girl worth chasing would be haunting the Horseshoe at one a.m. on Christmas morning. I sat down at Po's bar and the guy who called me Irish was working: he'd be there till five. He asked how long I was married. Seven years, I said. Any kids? Nah, I said. Jesus, that's crazy; I love kids; couldn't live without them. I nodded. He started to talk about his kids and I changed the subject to football. He took offence and walked away. Then suddenly I was up on my feet again and passing through the doors into the street outside, listening to loud piped Christmas music which was full of xylophone simplicity and sweet voices and the reassurance that one man loved us and suffered so that all men would be free. I was alone and drunk and five thousand miles from my house, and I could have crawled against a wall and slept for a week. I had nothing in my stomach.

I turned into the only spot I knew downtown where you could pay to see naked women – the Glitter Gulch. I'd never been inside: even the times I'd come with groups of guys, no one would enter. Ten years ago the outside was covered in hazy portraits of topless women posing temptingly. Now, as part of the attempted familification of downtown, all that was gone, including the guy outside who tried to lure you in.

In a dark sparse velvet-walled anteroom I paid the twenty-dollar cover. I could see the main stage from there. The woman dancing was old and unshapely, and there were only a handful of men watching. The air was oil-dark and loud – I think it was AC/DC. The girl behind the desk said, Thanks, enjoy yourself. I remember she had glitter all over her eyelids. Another woman, who was slightly haggish and sun-wrinkled and fat around the belly, took me by the arm and led me past thick black curtains. She asked me where I'd like to sit. The bar, I said. She asked if I'd like a dance and squeezed my arm and I realized she was offering. I told her I wanted to take it slow, which was not the truth.

The room was a large rectangle with a long bar in the middle. Green lights in the ceiling cast an atmosphere of radioactivity. It was not as empty as the first glance had suggested. There were several lone men at tables, some talking to dancers, others falling asleep. The girls were, for the most part, unsightly – some fat, some far too skinny, some wretchedly old and worn. The men were worse – they shined dismally in the green light and the roving white spotlights. They drank and flashed money. The girls came by and rubbed their shoulders and hair and whispered to them. Soon the dancers undressed and began to dance, asses on laps, arching backward, squeezing their tits together, making eye contact with other men. Meanwhile the girl on the main stage was nude and lying with her legs spread wide in front of some unenviable man, her fingers pulling her cunt open so that he could peer inside. On another part of the stage a woman hung upside down from a pole with her old tits dangling into her face. Here, yes, this was it, humanity like a cadaver, a cold corpse in a lab, cut open, ribs pulled out, organs dumped in a bin.

I sat at the bar, which was empty, and made friends with the bartender, Martin, a plump-faced, loquacious Latino who served me a beer for six dollars and a shot on the house. We talked for a long time about Ireland. He was taking advantage of the slow night to experiment with new cocktails, and we tried one after another – he made big ones for the girls and we drank the remainder in small glasses. During this time, which may have been half an hour, I wasn't approached by a single dancer. They walked past me as though I were a permanent fixture. I told Martin it was giving me a complex.

I can get one for you, he said.

But they're all fucking ugly, I said.

But, you know, it's Christmas morning.

And though it seems somewhat fibbish to say so, somewhat novelistic, it was around that time that a young, good-looking girl took a seat at the bar, about five spaces away, and ordered a drink. She had dark hair and white skin and started checking her phone. Martin made her something fruity and I told him I'd pay for it. When it came to her I called over, Can I join you?

Sure, she said.

Her name was Jackie. She had pretty, light-brown eyes and freckles. We made chit-chat – there seemed to be no rush. She was nineteen and studying literature at UNLV, or would continue as soon as she could afford to. Before she could afford to go to college she needed fake tits, so that she could work a little more and *really* afford to go to college. She missed her English courses. We got on to the subject of dead authors: her favourite Dostoevsky novels, Hemingway, several others that have slipped out of the grip of my memory. She said she wanted to become a writer. If she had not said that, I would've assumed the literary references were lies for my benefit, something out of a stripper handbook: how to talk to bookish men.

She said, Would you like a dance?

How much?

Here or in the private room?

The private room.

A hundred bucks for three songs, or three hundred for the hour.

Let's start with three songs, I said, because at the time it seemed the perfect balanced solution to the problem of this money: spend a hundred on Jackie, blow a hundred on roulette, and save a hundred for the morning.

She stood and took my hand and said, Follow me. Martin nodded – not ostentatiously, not creepily, but as though to say, See you in a bit. Jackie led me to a small space separated from the main room by dark but half-transparent curtains. In it was an L-shaped couch against the wall and a few tables. She picked a spot and sat down, crossed her legs, and lit a cigarette. Do you mind? she asked.

Not at all, I said. I lit a cigarette and leaned back into the seat and put my hand on her back. It was cool and muscular. She looked up, presumably at a camera, but said nothing.

What kind of stuff do you write? she asked.

All kinds of stuff.

A book?

Maybe.

She had her hand on my leg. I cannot remember if it had been there from the beginning. We were sitting in an odd calm that seemed a great distance from everybody else. We were all alone in the room. I have a tendency – and this is an old cliché but what can you do when it's the truth – to fall in love with strippers. I've never been to a club without leaving under a hazy, pathetic crush.

She tamped her cigarette in the ashtray. It was only half-smoked, but I understood. I did the same and leaned back and she put one leg over me and leaned forward. I put my hands on her waist and squeezed. I cannot even begin to express the sensation that contact with a woman's waist, the curve from the hips up, the soft flat belly, drives through me. It is like taking off all my clothes, standing in the rain, and grabbing an electric fence.

Dutifully Jackie threw her head back. She undressed when the next song began. She did this with the slow expertise of all strippers – this holding of the top against the breasts while the straps are undone, then the bent-over slow unravelling of a G-string – and in a moment she was naked on top of me, completely, faced away, and pressing her ass in my lap like a cat trying to get comfortable in a pillow. I scratched her back. She leaned forward and soon her hands were on the ground and she was upside down on my lap and I was staring into the eloquence of her hairless cunt and asshole. And I became something of that unenviable man, frozen, shaken, bankrupt. If I had been spotted by anyone they would have pitied me. When I pulled her ass apart with my hands she slid off with feline agility and moved to straddle me again and said, This is nice. If I had not been in love with her before, I was then. And if not then, I was when she danced into the fifth and sixth songs and when at last I could not bear to have her tits so close to my mouth without sucking them and I licked and bit her nipple and she squeezed herself close and let out an almost silent whimper.

Then she stopped and asked, Do you want to go longer? We've gone way past three songs.

I don't know, I said.

She remained very still.

Can I smoke a cigarette and think about it?

She got off my lap and put on her G-string and bikini top and lit a cigarette, reclining into the couch and crossing her legs. I'm probably going to get in trouble, she said. You're not supposed to touch me.

Yeah, but it's Christmas.

Exactly, it's Christmas.

We began a conversation again. She said she was tired, but had to dance the morning shift at a place on the Strip. That shift started at six, so she'd have a couple of hours to kill. I told her she should come back and drink with me at the Horseshoe. She thought about it. Maybe, she said.

Why do you want to get fake tits? I asked. Yours are perfect.

Hardly anybody likes real tits anymore, she said. You make a lot more if they don't move when you dance.

Well, I like them.

She put her cigarette in the ashtray. You want to see them again?

I want to fuck you.

She smiled. I'd *definitely* get in trouble.

Two hundred more for the rest of the hour?

She nodded. You should give Yuri something too.

Who's Yuri?

Yuri was the guy just outside the curtain who made sure the girls were safe, and that they didn't cross the line. I presumed Yuri was a fake name intended to intimidate clients, but he didn't need it. He was the shape of Frankenstein's monster. I gave Yuri fifty and he nodded without saying anything. I had no idea what value fifty bucks had in this economy, but when I told Jackie she raised her eyes and told me to move to the far corner of the couch.

I grabbed my cigarettes and slid to the far end of the L and she said, Okay, we're off camera.

When my time was up, it was about three a.m. There was another guy and his dancer, an older woman with short hair and cellulite, going through a conventional routine. He'd been watching us. We hadn't done anything too astonishing, but it had felt like sex. I felt like I'd been fucked. Jackie dressed and we went to the bar for a drink, and on the way out I gave Yuri another thirty dollars. I wanted to walk around the place giving everybody money.

At the bar, Martin was still experimenting with cocktails. We had a few shots – Jackie had shots and an energy drink – and my mouth began to fill with gobble and my tongue became chewing gum. I started lighting cigarettes and leaving them to burn in ashtrays. Jackie said she'd better try and make a little more money before her shift was finished. She had half an hour. I told her to come to the front bar of the Horseshoe – Po's bar – when she was done, and she said she would. When she left, Martin and I spoke until I could make no more sense of his words or my own. I went to stand and nearly fell over.

In an instant I was at the Horseshoe, at Po's bar, and the bartender said, Any luck, Irish? I said I was still losing, but was done for the night. I put twenty bucks in the quarter poker machine and pressed the button once. My free drink came. Beside me there was an old man who could speak only by pressing a bandaged-up hole in his throat, and even then you couldn't understand a word. At the end of the bar was a frat guy in a tattered baseball cap, dozing. There was one Asian dude playing roulette – the table that had crucified me – and one or two others playing blackjack. The craps dealers were standing silently in position while the pit boss paced behind them. The slots jingled in rhythmic alarm but I didn't see anyone playing them. It was four in the morning. I was drinking very slowly, and as the time passed and Jackie did not arrive, I grew sleepy. I closed my eyes a few times and may have dozed.

I was about to order some water and retire – I had to be up in a few hours to gamble with my father – when Jackie showed up. She was wearing jeans and red jumper with a low neckline, and flats. She sat down and said, I didn't think you'd be here.

I didn't think you'd come, I said.

So, do you really live in Ireland?

Yep.

Too bad, she said.

She began to play the poker machine at her seat. She had long fingernails and they cracked the buttons rapidly. She played with unconscious speed, and spoke at the same time.

She hit a big hand and won a few hundred dollars. The old guy started clapping and the frat guy woke up. The voice box spoke – it asked a question. I didn't understand but Jackie said, I got a flush. The old man nodded. He began to tell us a story about something. I didn't grasp a word of it. When he was finished he laughed very hard, and so did Jackie. The frat guy exploded momentarily about shit luck.

If you lived here, said Jackie to me, we could've given dating a shot.

I put my hand on her leg. The thought of dating someone who undressed and danced on top of other men filled me with lascivious curiosity. Dismissively, lightly scolding, she reminded me that I didn't live there, so there wasn't much point.

Did you think I was coming here to hook up with you?

Of course not, I said, instantly growing very tired.

The old man spoke again and Jackie responded. He's a writer, she said. He's going to write about us.

The old man turned and reached out to shake my hand. With his other hand he pushed his throat and said, Pleased to meet you.

We spoke, the three of us, Jackie translating, for another half-hour, suffering a few more explosions from the frat guy, who at one point began flexing his muscles and feeling them. He was totally oblivious to the moment. He could have been in a jungle hanging with apes. Finally Jackie said she had to go. She cashed out. She held my hand for a moment and kissed me. It was light but lingering – hard to say who did the lingering and who did the leaving. Then she walked out. The old man and I watched her. He said something. I didn't understand, but I knew what he said. I have a second memory of that morning, purely imaginary, in which she and I went up to my room and fucked and dozed through the day, and this imaginary memory is as true to my mind as what really happened – I could retell it now with the same sincerity. As she disappeared into the blinking, illuminated morning, she took all my energy with her. When she had vanished totally, the room became pendulous and swampy. My eyes began to close at once. My nose started to run again. The frat guy was talking about hookers. I knew what he meant. I told him to fuck off. The bartender said, It's Christmas, Irish, go get some rest.

Oakhurst, Texas

My mother lives in a small trailer on a couple acres of land that she and her husband, David, have turned into a little farm with vegetables and chickens and rabbits. To get there you have to cross a deep, muddy, litter-polluted gorge, and this cannot be done without a four-wheel-drive truck. It is a sinister-looking spot, the abandoned development where they live, just bulldozed roads that have turned, in a thousand heavy rains, to clay and slime. Everywhere you look there are hand-painted signs nailed to skinny pines that say Trespassers Will Be Shot, or DOG, and you are quite certain you'd rather be shot. Drive one minute up my mother's road and you find an empty two-storey house that used to be a meth lab. Part of it is collapsed, and a dozen cars rust outside it. My mother has lived in all sorts of places, but this is where she will die, someday, and I think she will die satisfied.

This is my second landscape, of muggy green woods and scrub pines and cut-out, semi-paved neighbourhoods. My second novel is about this place, but since it sits unfinished, memories remain and stir a great deal of lingering antipathy. Gas stations in the middle of nowhere. Long country highways narrowly forged out of unhealthy forests. Vast car dealerships, giant stores along the interstate, wide roads with closed-down groceries and industrial bottling complexes, colonies of chain restaurants at ten-lane intersections, creosote plants, pawn shops, sad diners with my mother, always working, always broke, who was, for a long time, the loneliest person on earth. But never defeated.

I arrived on the evening of the 27th. I don't remember the first night much. We saw a few relatives. We had dinner and a few beers and watched a movie, most of which I slept through. I woke the next day at around nine. It was warm and bright. My sheets were wet from night sweats and I felt better for it. My mother made coffee. We sat in front of the large television while she read a book about gardening and I read over a story I'd been meaning to edit – it had been accepted for publication, but I had to make some changes, make some connections more explicit. David was just up: he is a tall, white-haired man with short legs, hulking, monolithic and rectangular, except for his large belly. He is absurdly large in the situation of the tiny trailer. And he had looked better. He'd had cancers removed from his face, which was red and scabby – too many hours working outside, fixing roofs, rebuilding houses, and he hadn't the skin for it.

A Preparation for Death

We ate breakfast, a real feast – a dozen eggs hatched a hundred yards away and scrambled into very yellow huevos rancheros, a whole foot-long roll of ground country sausage fried in patties on an industrial skillet, a loaf of toast. I still didn't have an appetite, and my mother looked upon my plate with disappointment, suggesting, without a word, that I had grown too skinny. It was true, and I could see my mother was weighing the risks of approaching the matter. No doubt the first sight of me in a year had been shocking: thin and green-grey, suddenly bald after quitting medication, and bird-legged. After breakfast, I gave my mother something of mine to read – a new essay just published in an Irish journal. I hoped, perhaps, that it might speak to my new attitude toward intent, my lucky torment – the lucid and lyrical substance of flesh in mid-rot, a song of self in dissolution. She read too silently, so I went for a shower. I checked myself in the mirror. I examined my body. The muscles in my arms were gone. I flexed and became winded. When I was out of the shower my mother said nothing of the essay, except, Have you started smoking?

We had some more coffee on the back porch, a wooden platform David built that is as wide and nearly as long as the trailer. From it, the yard drifts downward. A garden, an old barn, a greenhouse, another road. Little interrupts the serenity. A flushed toilet, and the shallow sewage lines gurgle toward the septic tank. Gunshots. Dogs barking or howling. From time to time a neighbour flies up or down the road in his battered Suzuki SUV, a fourteen-year-old on thrill rides. He, Dustin, who is my size but doughy and boyish, has no father and his mother is in jail for selling crack. He lives with his grandparents. He's got no friends. He explodes fireworks and shoots inanimate objects. He paid us a short visit nearly every day, mainly to eat scraps and tell nigger jokes – he was, quite obviously, half black, but his grandparents told him he just tanned well. When he went by that morning he honked and my mother waved.

The sun was out but the day was hazy. A chicken hawk began to circle and my mother screamed at it a dozen times to get the hell away – she speaks with animals. It hid on a treetop and my mother shrieked, I see you, you sonofabitch! It shot off. When enough time had passed and it had not come back, we let the chickens out and fed them carrots. You hold the stalks tightly and let them peck, and when there is not much left they peck your fists and wrists. They are immensely healthy-looking animals – glossy and fat. Very calm, for chickens. Sometimes one hops on your leg, or shoulder, and squats for a while like an aloof and overweight potentate. When they had eaten all they wanted, we fed the rabbits.

I watched my mother tend her garden. The chickens followed her like lieutenants attending a contemplative general around a tent on the eve of battle. She is both sad and youthful, like a lovesick teenager. I know that she has regrets. I dream that I may somehow make up for the potential she threw away – she was endlessly creative and intelligent, but she sacrificed. The story is an old one, but your mother is your mother. You love her pain like you love your own. The blonde colouring in her hair was old, and an inch of grey roots was showing. She wears thick glasses because her work, refurbishing houses with David, is too messy for contacts.

My mother has always been at home around violence. She has, from time to time, a maniacal blood-temperature. Once, our cat, a poor, declawed thing we transplanted from San Antonio to

Conroe after the divorce, was killed by a handful of Dobermann pinschers that belonged to a neighbour. They were in the middle of eating it when my mother walked up behind them with a .357 and, without shouting, not angrily, shot two of those dogs. She called the neighbour and told him to come pick them up. When he threatened to call the police, she dared him to. He relented. Another time, when I was eleven or twelve, a cousin hid a bag of weed under my bed. In the middle of some night he crawled through my window to retrieve it – but it had already been discovered. My mother woke and called him into the living room. She beat and bloodied him with her bare fists. Years before that, at a youth soccer game in San Antonio, some father got irate about some penalty, and ran to his truck to get a weapon – in my memory it was a crowbar. Everybody scattered but my mother. She stood between the man and the referee and told him if he hit her, he had better kill her, because she would chase him to the ends of the earth and get revenge. Not one man came to that referee's aid.

Her work selling insurance, after the divorce, took her to far-flung homes in the rural wastelands of east Texas, and sometimes I went with her. We often encountered frothing and outraged guard dogs. They would gnaw on fence posts as she approached – I was too afraid to leave the car, but she would step through the gate, kneel, speak to the dog, and at once it would fall under some spell of love and pacification. The owners would say, I've never seen anything like that. Soon the dogs would be lying at her feet, and the owners would be writing cheques. I try to remind her of these things, and she pretends they never happened.

The last time I visited, we took David's guns out – he has

dozens: pistols, shotguns, rifles – and shot at targets in a junked-out section of the farm. My mother sat on a frayed folding chair and held the ammunition, drinking iced tea. It was bright and muggy. David and I were all pretty bad shots, and my mother made mock-encouraging remarks when we missed. David said, Okay, Frances, let's see what you can do. She took the rifle, complained about the glare, hitched into a forward-leaning stance, and hit everything. The beer cans we had placed on tree trunks and cardboard boxes flipped and bounced and tumbled off their perches, one after another. I guess we'll have to move them farther back, she said.

The subject of the end of my marriage was avoided until it could no longer be, and later that day, perhaps it was the evening, I delivered a brief and abridged confession of my sins. She listened with a studied dread, nodding at times but mostly still. Reliving past horrors, I suppose. If I had thought about it, I would've abridged the story further, though it was already more of an excuse than a confession. I had been forthright with everybody else. I desired contempt, because I was beyond it, so great was my self-loathing. But with my mother I merely wanted it over.

I had caused her enough pain already. Between the eighth and ninth grades, I left her and Conroe to live with my father in San Antonio. I withdrew myself from her life at a time when she had nothing but an ignorant and loud-mouthed second husband and a family that was too religious to console her. It is easy to excuse the cruelties of children, since they cannot comprehend the weight of them on other people, but I have always understood and used the weakness others have for me. Though she is considerably more content with herself now, and with David, she has harboured the belief that I left because I loved my father more than her.

At the time, she knew I was in trouble at school, failing classes, getting in fights, but she did not know the extent of things. I was getting my ass kicked almost every day. And when I was not getting my ass kicked, I was hurrying from classroom to classroom, taking back-routes, trying to keep out of sight. All this came about, or at least began, because of something I said. One day during an off-season football practice – we were, in fact, playing baseball – I, without thinking, using a term my uncles used to refer to me, called a black kid *boy*. Perhaps I knew what it meant and used it anyway. If I was a racist then, I wasn't aware of it. He punched me without any conversation, no taunts or intimidation. It was a jab that caught me on the cheek. There was a jolt, but it had not hurt – that struck me as totally impossible. Thinking of it now – no wonder, he was a few inches shorter than me and not as broad, and he was thirteen. Nevertheless I was terrified. A coach, from the other side of the field, told the black kid to leave me alone, not out of concern for my safety but because I was a puny waste of time: if you're going to fight, he told the kid, pick somebody who'll give you one. Nevertheless, the kid attacked me again. He punched me six or seven times. I was too scared to run, and I never raised a hand to defend myself, not even to cover my face. The kid walked away to finish the game. I hoped he had bored himself. I remember pins and needles in my arms and legs, not from fear, not precisely, but from a realization a thousand times more abominable – that I had not considered, and wouldn't consider, the possibility of punching him back.

When the game ended he came at me once more. Again I did

nothing. For about a week this continued. I'd be ambushed by fifty students who wanted to see the spectacle of the Boy Who Would Not Fight. The black kid eventually tired of giving me beatings, but just as soon as that crisis had gone by, another ten started. It had become obvious to everybody that I would not raise a hand against them. For months I was a punching bag, and humiliatingly it was almost always by boys smaller than me. Large galleries watched like a talk-show audience, just laughing, coaxing. Once, in a scene reminiscent of a gruesome Mafia dock-lands execution, three kids – this time they were much bigger – led me to an isolated spot, far behind the football field, in the middle of a school day, to beat me up. I did not beg or whimper, but I did not struggle either, nor try to run away. They began to push me around. While the ringleader watched, the other two tried to incite me. Ten minutes passed. The leader asked me if I knew why it was happening. I said nothing. I had stopped wondering what the reason was; all that consumed me was my inability to respond. These fights took place wholly within me. The two lost interest, but the third grew so angry at my inaction that he struck me anyway, just once. That too did not hurt, but I shat myself. A hard and giant turd, cleanly, was in my underwear. After they walked away, I pulled my jeans down, lifted it out in my palm, and left it in the street.

The vice-principal, in his office, once told me, For God's sake, defend yourself! I told him I didn't want to get detention. *Detention!* He slapped his forehead. On a weekend trip to San Antonio, that summer, I told my father I wanted to move in with him. He told my mother. Cowardice after cowardice after cowardice. And even now, back in east Texas, I am whipped, now and then, by a paroxysm of those memories. Sometimes I begin to perspire and must get up and walk. If not for my mother, I would never come back here. I would never drive through. I would never take a flight that flew over. In San Antonio, entering high school, I decided to stick up for myself, not because I wanted to, but because the truth of my nature was too tight around my neck. I got in a few fights, which did not last long, just to get over the fear of punching. Then I joined the swim team, grew a few inches, and nobody wanted to fight anymore. I used to lie in bed some nights and dream of killing. I still do. When I think of it, my heart grows lusty. I would like to beat someone to his death. Just to get the cowardice out of me.

On the evening of the 28th, my cousin Chris arrived. We were out back drinking beer in the warm night, and it seemed that we heard him from a very long way off: a high-pitched four-cylinder whine – overworked, threatening to evaporate – shattered the high countryside quiet, the silence over the treetops. It had rained for many days before I arrived, and the roads should have been impassable for a two-wheel-drive, but my mother explained that Chris simply buries the gas and flies down the gorge and up it.

It had been years. We shook hands – his hands are gigantic, almost cartoonish, like his father's. He wore amber Ray-Bans. We put a few extra chairs in the living room, and we were all on top of each other. Chris and I were nearly the same person for a long time, when I first moved to Conroe. I was in the fifth grade and he was in the seventh, and we went to different schools, but we spent every evening and weekend together. He hated school and would never finish. He was an inventor, and took apart and rebuilt electronic devices – radios, microwaves, televisions – and drew schematic diagrams to understand them. If someone had figured out a way to interest him in school, he'd have become a professor. But now he installs car radios in a small Texas town, and talks without conviction of a plan to start his own business. I would like to say this doesn't disappoint me, that one life is as admirable – or pointless – as the next, but sitting with him while he drank coffee and talked about his sick child and his plans to install a new septic tank I was reminded of the hopeless dreams and phantasmagoria of our childhoods – another old story, but how poignant they seem to us when we are made of them. He left after a third phone call from his impatient wife, and we heard him struggling up the gorge, and the high-pitched whine of the engine trailed away.

Later that night I took my computer out to work on edits to my story. David put on some music, something called *Celtic Woman*. He'd seen the ad on television and called the phone number. I tried to force it out of my consciousness. My mother picked up the magazine with my essay in it, scanning it again.

Do you mean everything you say in it? she asked.

I suppose, I said.

She frowned. She told me I was, as a child, always badly hurt by the insults of other children, that I was predisposed to long sulks and grudges. And it made her sad to see so many heads in the pillories of my unhappy onslaughts. It seemed too much like revenge to her. I felt it was the opposite of revenge – or that if revenge it was, the actors had enacted it upon themselves. My wrath was not directed at them but at myself for idolizing kings and princes of a corrupt world. I had, at last, and for good, cast myself into exile.

She remained suspicious. After all, I was rewriting, right in front of her, a story for publication in the US. I had explained to her, earlier, that I disagreed with the edits – I'd been asked to transform a story only I could write into a story anybody could've written. I was adding motivation, explanation, blatancy, all to confirm the editor's presumptions.

But I am finished fighting. To commit an act of violence on art or abandon it: it is the same thing. I want to eliminate art from my concerns, so that I rid myself of small thoughts. I will live and create wholly. A man who does this – and perhaps I will never be this man – re-emerges from the fraudulence and carnage asymmetrical, ugly, and contradictory, and lives as a totality, himself. I love the disfigured, the monstrous. All the books I admire are ogres – flawed, imbalanced, savage. They enhance me. Everything else reduces me.

Hartsfield International, Atlanta (II)

My last six hours in America were spent at a bar in Terminal A, right next to the gate for San José, Costa Rica, as though I needed a reminder of the world's cyclical nature. I waited hopefully for Jake, but he never showed. My flight was at eight, so I'd miss the New Year. I suspected, for no reason whatsoever, that there'd be a party on the plane. But in case there was none, I was having my party at the bar. Midnight in Dublin was seven o'clock in Atlanta. I convinced the bartender and a few of the people beside me – two were Irish, on their way to Costa Rica – to count down to seven o'clock. The bartender was beautifully flirtatious about everything. She told me she liked working in airport bars better than bars in the city. She loved to see the people go by. We had no champagne, so she poured soda water into cheap white wine, as I suggested.

The hours passed rapidly. People surfaced and sank. A girl my age from Canada sat beside me for a while. She read my palm. She was drunk, and spoke with her face very close to mine. A Costa Rican man gave me his card, and told me to come visit him. A businessman returning from Germany told a story that nearly put me to sleep. At seven, we, whatever congregation of travellers we were, counted down loudly from ten. Nobody had the same time, so we picked a moment out of thin air. The people in the gates around us, waiting, stopped what they were doing to observe.

6

The Sound of Water on a Body

1

It was the end of April, not suddenly, not gradually: a taxi, some night, and the air was full of raindrops – tiny magnifications of city light calcifying over Dame Street, and they did not even seem to be falling. I was rolling past the Central Bank. Along the footpath pedestrians hailed the emptiness, all drunk, some standing in the middle of the street. It was three a.m. I cracked the window and the mist spat in – either that or get sick. I moved in and out of consciousness. It was entirely true that I was the dream of somebody no longer alive.

The driver, who said nothing, went out of his way to stop at yellow lights. A few times he braked so violently I had to catch my food from sliding off the seat. The radio played country, and this seemed to utterly dissociate the car from the night, as though we were not at all on the road but a maid on a pig flying over the moon – and just like that I was the dream of Bulgakov, whom I had been reading. The sensation was over before I knew it. We slowed at a roundabout, and the car was on the road again.

I am many dreams. The new year is one. The city is another. My office. A room in the Irish Writers' Centre. Some days I am my gargling Vespa, floating past traffic down Capel Street. Other days I am the 128 bus – jammed on Amiens Street like a crooked headstone in an old, overcrowded cemetery. I am the days that elongate at their edges, heading for summer. I am the dream of a thousand wretched little houses, my cramped and hideous estate. I am the books I teach, and the stories of my students. I am not separate from these things, nor within them. I am not above or behind myself. I am what I sense.

I've been taking the bus more often. My scooter was stolen, wrecked, and recovered, and is in and out of the shop – the mechanics and I are arguing over the definition of a wobble. I live beside the terminus – a yellow pole stuck in some gravel by a cul-de-sac, surrounded by cranes, an empty, half-finished office installation, temporary walls, rubbish, and other construction – so I get my pick of seats. I bury myself in reading for an hour – I am gone – and when I see the Custom House I pack everything into my bag, turn on some music, and wait for my stop.

2

In the park beside St Patrick's Cathedral, where junkies and the homeless assemble among bright manicured flowers and green lawns, and parents bring children to play beside the fountains, I met Clare and we drank a few bottles of beer out of a paper bag. I'd come straight from work – all week I'd done nothing but watch little tasks go by – and found her on a bench, legs crossed, reading a short story, looking like she was born for such distractions. It was Friday, and she wore a yellow coat and large, black, square sunglasses. I sat down and put my hand between her thighs. This was the first time we had met like this, but there wasn't much point taking it slowly, since it wasn't going to last long. She hoped to enjoy some of the cool sunshine, but by the time I arrived it was cloudy and windy. There was a ladder in her black, translucent stockings. Oh well, she said, opening one of the beers. She is blonde and small – five foot two or three, yet somehow terribly formidable – and though she is beyond the petty obsessions of her own happiness and unhappiness, she has very pretty green-blue eyes that turn downward, and this gives her a constant expression of suffering someone else's loss. She has a PhD in economics and a crooked front tooth.

By the time the beer was finished, the cloudy light had cast a dullness over everything. The cool months had become exasperating – not winter, not spring, not anything. We went to a pub across the road and sat on stools because all the tables were taken. Clare wore a green-and-white dress that was tight around her waist. We had known each other for many months, but I'd only just discovered her attraction to me – she did not seem like the kind of woman who'd be interested. I remember nothing of the conversation except my surprise that it was taking place. Later we kissed inside a lifeless, unadorned pizza-slice kiosk with a Polish man in a white hat behind the counter, talking on his mobile phone.

3

It takes forever to get anywhere now. The city is overrun – tourist season has begun. The streets you hardly notice are suddenly worth a million photographs.

The enthusiasm of the tourists depresses me, because it makes me think of the tedium of wherever they are from. I think of a single civilization linked by grey intersections and manicured parks, and the world becomes inescapable – its inescapability is a fact.

There are too many days in the week. Too many weeks in the year. Too much space to fill. I would like to have lived for an afternoon only, born at the age of twenty, dead eight hours later, experienced life, all by myself, in a corner apartment with a high view of a busy junction, an ambulance route, a metro entrance, the back of a restaurant, warring neighbours in the corridors, a broken television, an empty bookshelf, and learned only sensitivity, because I would have missed nothing, gained the same experience of life, and would not have grown so addicted to existence that the thought of not existing gives me indigestion and bad dreams.

He who has learned to die has unlearned how to be a slave. [Montaigne]

But I am like anyone else – fear and apprehension rule many of my hours. And addiction to the dispensable. Because it is more agreeable to be in bondage to the superficial, and have a thing or two in common with the man sitting beside you on the bus – whose acts are repetitions, whose memories are souvenirs, whose entertainment is palatable – than to become incomprehensible.

Never did a man prepare to leave the world more utterly and completely, nor detach himself from it more universally, than I propose to do. [Montaigne]

I want to peel my skin off with my fingernails, nail it down, batter it with a mallet until it is the consistency of stomach, and

99

wrap it around every shaft and every curve and every angle of every letter in this sentence. I want this sentence to forgive me. Instead, it becomes a reminder of my incapability as a man.

4

This morning, while sitting on a bench in the grounds of Dublin Castle, eating one of the sandwiches I made at home, I took in some sun while other reporters chased doctors around: between the keynote speaker and the first panel discussion, there was a twenty-minute coffee break. The fraternity of eminent Irish cancer specialists had gathered – Hollywood, Reynolds, Lawler, Keane, Armstrong – to deliver updates and arguments to a banquet hall full of empty chairs and half a dozen journalists. After the keynote speech, the organizer addressed us all – thank you for contributing to one of the largest conferences in our history, he said. During the Q&A afterwards, a woman in a white suit with large, freckled, sunburned cleavage and unnecessarily high heels dashed around with a microphone, though all the questions came from one very annoying woman and one very annoying man – and they were not even questions, just noise. When it finished, I found a free bench in the courtyard. The doctors watched me leave with disappointment – how could they pretend to want to avoid the press, if the press was going to decamp? But it was not contempt for them – I have no feelings personally toward them – but for my own unpreparedness for death. And the loathing for the whole race that quickens in me, listening to its obsession with survival.

5

I am the dream of what I see, now, from a folding metal chair on my terrace: gigantic white clouds, moving fast toward the sea. Above the sea, they are slate-coloured, the colour of glaciers. Rooftops to my right. To my left, a cluttered dining room and kitchen. A dead strawberry plant that belongs to Helen. A gathering of pathetic vegetation, including an overgrown rosemary bush, and three pots of dirt. It is a Saturday, and the estate is empty. I haven't heard a person walking all morning, or a car drive by. By now – it is noon – the neighbourhood kids should be drinking and smoking in my driveway. It is better to let them. Helen found herself a handsome boyfriend and is never around anymore. The other day she told me she plans to move out in a month – I live too far away from the city. Katie, who moved in briefly, has left to live with a musician friend in Smithfield. If she were here, she'd be playing the fiddle downstairs, in the room she slept in, which has no bed. I'm listening to Niel Gow to make up for her absence. My vision of a summer with two pretty twentysomething girls with funny accents sunning on my terrace is gone. The washing machine, from time to time, spins and drowns everything out. Now it is beeping. It is time to hang up my boring blue shirts.

6

Yesterday at the office I checked email: Clare had been overjoyed by the sight of a tall woman and a dwarf smoking cigarettes outside a pub – the dwarf was standing on a short wall, so they were the same height. Katie's life in the city, playing sessions every night, was wonderful, but she missed the acoustics in my house. John was flying to Prague for a stag – that man surrounds himself with trouble. Some students had questions about assignments. At ten to one I ate my sandwiches, and at one I left the office for my work local, and read two stories by new students. I had a short chat with the bartender, a fat and wise and irascible and lazy man who is always stoned. At two, I was back at my desk. My list of things to do seemed longer, but only because I now had half a day to accomplish them. Outside, the weather changed, and the bright clear day was suddenly full of hail and wind and darkness.

The deputy editor, Mary Anne, who is two years younger than me, stared out the window contemplatively. It was almost time to go, and she – like all of us – would get caught in it. Sometimes she is pretty, and sometimes she is exceptionally pretty. She is pale with large blue eyes and her cheeks go bright red for no reason that I know of. She wears skirts and has beautiful legs, which move slowly and luxuriously under her desk when she is concentrating – and when I notice this happening I spend the next few minutes being the dream of her high patent-leather grey heels.

7

On the first warm day of the year, Clare and I took the Dart to Howth. The walk from my house to Howth Junction winds through two bleakly repetitive estates. I don't mind the vulgarity of suburbs, only my imprisonment in one. I don't hate peace and quiet, or children, just my proximity to them.

Clare is a constant anthropologist. Her mind is always decoding her surroundings. Sometimes this leads her to outlandish conclusions, and experimental solutions to the problem of suburbs, such as destroying them all. I sense that she is great company for herself, and that other people tend to get in the way. She walks twice as fast as me, and admits that she does so because she is small, and doesn't like to slow tall people down.

I had hoped that we might have a bit of seaside to ourselves, but Howth was swarmed with day trippers, particularly foreigners: eastern Europeans, Italians, Americans, Germans. Outside the station, traffic was jammed in both directions. The bar underneath the station was overrun – people were sitting in windows and on rails; it was like a third-world train carriage. There was a posh market selling cheeses and jams and jewellery. I saw a French flag and heard some accordion music. It was as busy as a city street at rush hour, except no one was in a hurry. Everyone was in shorts and sunglasses. We headed toward the yacht club, an ugly yellow pentagonal building, to look at some of the sailboats docked in the marina. Sailboats are a kind of aphrodisiac to Clare. The fact that I crew for a boat in Dun Laoghaire – this is a remnant of my old life – makes the sight of them that much more alluring, since she feels that if only we could get our hands on a small dinghy, I could sail her around Ireland. But it was low tide, and the marina was full of sludge and stank of sea-fish. And a soccer game that seemed to have neither goals nor boundaries had usurped all the nice places to sit.

We walked a little further. For a little while we lay on a patch of grass so I could try to sleep. I was badly hungover. Beside us, people in shorts and flip-flops mobbed the pier. And though I could not sleep – I can hardly ever sleep – I closed my eyes and put my hands on Clare's belly, which is soft and flat and white, and has a few moles on it.

I tend to idle with anxiety – I always feel that I'm forgetting something. Clare idles with a nonchalance so stylish that it borders on the professional. It is as though she could sit still, admiring her own contentment, during an earthquake.

We hiked up Howth Head to avoid drinking too early. I had seen it from the sea many times. It is dark green and gorse-patched, with sheer rock cliffs. When you are on a boat, the head seems merely large, but when you are looking from the head to the water, you feel as though you're on a mountain, and that a gust might throw you to your death. That day the sea was calm and the waves bashed the rocks quietly. We walked beside each other when the path was wide enough, and single file when it narrowed. We passed a woman with a video camera. She was filming the sea while talking to a friend: the camera would experience the moment for her.

We had a pint outside a small hotel in Howth village. A group of drunk English tourists were shouting and drinking cider in the last hour or two of high sunlight, sunlight still above the rooftops opposite. They were all very sunburned and this made them feel beautiful. The men wore unbuttoned shirts and the women wore white trousers. One woman, sitting down, suddenly fell into the bushes.

We took a late train back home – it was filled with the same crowds that had come out with us, but now they were slumbering – and had some wine on the terrace. Summer had arrived. I was disconsolate: the world was unstoppable. We went to bed and she undressed. I kept my clothes on for a few minutes and examined every inch of her. I put my hands around her throat. She has large soft breasts, and they flatten when she is on her back. She has multiple orgasms and goes limp for a while after them.

The next day, after breakfast and coffee, we sat on the terrace again – there is nowhere else one would sit in pleasant weather – and she sat on my lap and we kissed in the sunlight. The whole thing – the first warmth of the year, breakfast outside, the sound of airplanes – aroused her so much that she gave me head in plain sight of the third-storey windows across the street, all open. We spent the afternoon in bed. She came again and again, and slept, and I scratched her back and bottom while she slept. I felt, that day, that I was twenty-one again, and no part of the past decade had taken place.

8

I am going to miss Helen much more than she knows. She has become an ersatz wife. She is messy and poor, and has no inter-est in chit-chat. If I liked her music, I would throw myself at her feet and beg her to love me. Instead we operate in proximity but separately.

It is delightful to watch her morning rituals. Since she works different hours every week, I catch different episodes of it. And sometimes on weekends, if I am up writing, I can observe it entirely. It begins like a single bee sucking nectar out of a flower, delightful, beautiful, delicate, and gradually others arrive, until suddenly the sky is black with a swarm of them.

She wakes more than two hours before she must leave the house – the intent is to finally, for once in her life, not be late. First she goes upstairs to the kitchen and dining room, makes a cup of tea, and reads a book. She has good taste in books, and a broad appetite. She sits on a chair at the kitchen table, knees pulled up to her chin, and holds the book at a distance, sipping her tea, black, never removing the bag. Because the weather is warmer, she wears a vest top and boxers – in the winter she wore a thick black hooded jumper and check pyjama bottoms. Either way she is rather exquisite – not merely pretty but perfectly calm. When her tea is finished she goes downstairs to take a shower. This is where her schedule falls apart. She takes showers that last forty minutes. She says it is because she has lots of hair and must wash it completely. Sometimes she must wash it twice. The idea of her washing her hair for such a long time suffuses me with calm. I imagine she must wash every strand. I imagine she has no thoughts at all – that she becomes nothing more than the sound of a woman washing her hair, the sound of water on a body. When she emerges, she returns to the kitchen to read more and have another cup of tea and breakfast, which is usually a piece of toast. She already knows she will be late, but she must have peace with breakfast. Her hair is wet and thick and very black, and there are times I have wanted to put my hands on it – if only to lower my heart rate. Again she falls into a silence. When she is in this state, one must not speak to her. One feels that to make noise would be to shatter something precious. Then she will check her phone for the time, and slowly the swarm begins to gather. She jogs downstairs to put on make-up. This always takes longer than she expects, and then she must dry her hair. Because there is no socket in the bathroom, and no mirrors anywhere else but in the bathroom, she stands in front of the upstairs window – she has run upstairs – with a blow-dryer and a comb and watches herself in the reflection of the glass. She is always, at this stage, in a vest top and jeans or a skirt. She has a short tartan skirt that makes me feel like a paedophile. Her waist is nothing. I could reach around it with two hands – touching my thumbs and fingertips. The drying takes forever. Her hair comes down to the middle of her back. The repetition of combing and drying is slow and patient, but after fifteen minutes it becomes erratic, and she is full of sighs, and threatens to shave it all off. If I am watching, she asks me what time it is every minute. She never quite finishes – she always only has five minutes left, and there are still a million things to do. From then, it is all panic, running, stomping, doors slamming behind her, until a voice calls distantly from below, Goodbye! Then the front door shuts and she flies silently to the bus stop, and the air is empty again.

9

A new beginners course began tonight – a Thursday, mid-May – and now I am home after four straight nights of teaching. It is almost midnight. Helen has left an open bottle of red wine in the fridge. It tastes like cold, sour raspberries. I am too tired to write. My brain is exhausted. It is like this every night. I would like to say everything, but I can't think to remember any of it. I will go downstairs and sleep without reading. The corpse of what I could say now, if I had the energy, tumbles into lost time, on top of all the others.

10

The clouds are a hundred shades of grey. It is like being in the centre of a nebula. You could spend your whole life staring upwards in Texas, and never see anything like them.

11

The future is a city. And I am the dream of a man who died in it. But I am also the dream that murdered that man.

12

A man who writes loves his city more than his own life or death – a failed writer all the more. The city inspires him, but refuses to belong to him. It endures all his nonsense. It does not requite his obsession.

In the evenings after class, after drinks, I wait for the bus at the bottom of O'Connell Street, on Eden Quay. The stop is just outside a lap-dancing club, the Garden of Eden, and patrons – fat foreign men in scuffed leather jackets and necklaces – tiptoe in and out. I am going in, as soon as I can afford to. The daylight is unimaginable now – almost five years in Ireland and I still cannot get used to it – and even at eleven there is still a little blue in the sky. The north quays toward Connolly Station – this is how half the city goes home – are frenetic. Cars honk their horns, but nobody cares. Last night, a Monday night, the moon was gold and shining in a sheet of haze. I can't afford cigarettes, but I am still buying them. I've decided to cut back on dinner, and just eat sandwiches for the rest of my life. Passengers gather at the bus stop. Ten minutes pass, fifteen. Buses mass at the light on Westmoreland Street, across the bridge. I squint to read their numbers – none of them are mine. The light goes green and they trot up O'Connell Street like fat cattle. I tell myself that this is experience, this waiting.

13

I met Clare for dinner on Dame Street. I came straight from class, which had run twenty minutes late. I felt bad, but had forgotten that Clare likes moments on her own. She hadn't even noticed. The weather was grey again, and when the late-lit nights in summer are full of uncertain rain – rain that begins when you take your hood down, and stops when you lift it up – and gusts of wind, and suddenly cool again, the city has the feel of apocalypse about it.

When I arrived at the restaurant – a small and deliberately untidy spot that serves big cheap archetype mains: lamb stew, roast chicken, beef Bourguignon – Clare was seated at the very back, in an emerald-green top and an amber-coloured costume necklace, hair pulled back, reading. I was badly ravelled – none of my thoughts would dissipate, or retreat into unconscious space. It is always like this. They sardine together in a room and speak at the same volume. So she spoke about herself for a while and I listened. She had been working at a conference all week – hundreds of countries had gathered to ban cluster bombs. This seemed more important than my headache. I drank some wine. Slowly I came out of myself, and it was wonderful to be eating dinner in the city on a weeknight. And all the better since I could not afford it. The restaurant emptied. It grew dark, finally, and began to rain with equanimity.

After dinner, we went to a Russian wine bar on Wicklow Street. I'd been on beer heavily for the previous three nights and could not fit any more bubbles. Inside, there was a man playing muzak on a saxophone, sad and sexy versions of Europop. There was a tall woman with a beautiful and skinny body, but then we saw that she was not at all pretty. Next to us, an old foreign man began singing to his female companion. She inched away from him, and he swallowed her up in his arms. His mouth was so wide open as he sang that I thought he might try to fit her head inside it, and eat her like a snake eats a rat.

When the wine was finished, we walked to Clare's flat, which she shares with another girl. It is tiny, clean but city-centre-grimy – old carpets, mildew in the bathroom, gunk in the sink, the smell of rental living. The ceilings are low, the windows are single-glazed. I feel thoroughly pleased by it, thinking of what is to become of me, once I sell the house. Weak showers. Small, squeaky beds. Ice-cold rooms in winter, sleeping by electric heaters. A room with a small desk. My books will overcrowd the room.

14

Clare's room, which is a yellow rectangle, has interesting but forgettable prints on the walls, a bookshelf that is neatly decorated with things she has gathered on her travels and a great deal of costume jewellery, a small bed beside which are piled the many new books she has bought in a jagged and unstable chimney stack. There is a mirror beside her bed, in front of which she does her make-up, and in which I am always watching ourselves in bed – I love to watch the way she desires to be fucked, her at-homeness in desire. Nothing is beyond her. I wish we were in love. Her closets are so overstuffed with outfits and coats that she must hang things everywhere. But she spends very little time in her apartment, only to sleep, bathe, and watch videos. She likes to read outdoors, or in pubs, and eat in inexpensive cafés. She lives in the city. She takes up all of it.

My house is tall and narrow. The bottom two floors are like the bowels of a ship. Everything is tight and poorly lit. I don't even use the bedroom on the first floor, which was – what a long time ago that seems, but only a year – my study. Now it holds a few books, some winter coats, and an American football. The second floor has two bedrooms, one – mine – an ensuite, and a large bathroom, which is Helen's, but I shave there, since my bathroom lacks a mirror. My bedroom is large, but so is the bed, so there is not much room. There are some old papers and a cluttered closet where nothing is folded, merely thrown in bunches gathered off the clothes horse. I have a few books stacked on the window sill. The shower has no shield – just a box cut out of the wall. The bathroom floor is streaked with stains and dirt. The sink is festering in soap scum. The toilet is filthy.

15

My bosses think I hide behind apathy, and that is why I'm going nowhere in journalism. But it is through apathy that I endure journalism.

It has become the understood thing that no one can live by his talents or knowledge who is not ready to prostitute those talents and that knowledge to betray his species, and prey upon his fellow man. [Hazlitt]

I will squander whatever I can make of journalism.

In the evenings, teaching, my apathy becomes mania. It is like my skin is yanked inside out. My repudiation finds something worth talking about, and is armed with the pieces of writing I give to students to read, salvos that, momentarily, reverse the flow of civilization: Gogol, Maupassant, Dostoevsky, Chekhov, Schulz, Kafka, Borges, Conrad, Augustine, Baldwin, Orwell, Woolf, Faulkner, Bunin, Miller, Seneca, Plutarch, Kharms, Tanizaki, Lu Hsun, Kenko, Nietzsche, Mansfield, Cioran, Montaigne. Whatever society degrades, a genius ennobles; whatever society embraces, a genius obliterates. It makes my heart clamour now just to think of them. We gather around a few mismatched tables in a small, green-grey second-floor room with windows that look south over the gravity of excess and wealth. We are the enraptured state of failure.

But here I am talking about geniuses, and savages, at midnight, at my dining-room table, drinking tea, wearing two jumpers because it is cold again and has rained all day.

16

After a short heatwave that had everyone in T-shirts and lunching on the Liffey boardwalk, the city grew cool and grouchy. Coats and umbrellas returned. For two days the drop in temperature brought the most fantastic heavy fog into the city. It altered the nature of everything. Pedestrians, cars, motorcycles – they were all like ghost ships. The tops of buildings evaporated. And in this reorganization my acuity became so over-enhanced that every image, every sound, became the overflowing bulk of the proof and contradiction of the proof of perception, of the act of perceiving, and the solidity and liquidity of meaning. And I wanted nothing from this equilibrium but to live in it for a while.

The fog broke in the late evening of the second day. After class I skipped drinks to bus home and get some sleep. At a quarter past nine there was still a lot of muted daylight. But it seemed to come from nowhere. We rumbled up the Malahide Road in a torpor. I put away the assignments I was trying to mark and turned my music up very loud – Piaf. What an ability to render herself. I don't understand a word of it. I don't want to.

17

Clare and I came to my house after abandoning a Saturday night early – we had been kissing in crowded bars and when I lifted her dress in a half-crowded alleyway and pulled the crotch of her underwear to one side, she decided it was time to go. She was in a soft and tight blue-and-white dress with long sleeves and a low neck. Every time I see her she is wearing a new outfit – she has a great knack for finding unusual things that look good on her. She tells me she can go a year without wearing the same thing twice. And I have seen her room, which is like a wardrobe closet on a movie set, so I believe her. We got a taxi and I put my hand up her dress and she closed her eyes and spread her legs open and leaned her head back, and the taxi man saw this without really looking; after a few minutes of politenesses he shut up. I moved her underwear and put a finger inside her. She was very wet, and the smell of her filled the taxi. The driver opened a window. My mind had opened like a large mouth. Blind and bottom-feeding.

We got out and I had trouble unlocking my door because Clare was behind me with a hand down my jeans. We stepped inside and I put her on the staircase and unzipped my jeans and lifted her dress and pulled her underwear off and fucked her. She came immediately as I entered her. She was so wet it was like fucking in mud. It was coming down my legs, pooling on the staircase. I told her I was going to come inside her; she nodded. Come inside me, she said. I came. I could feel the head of my dick pressed into her cervix, and I fed every drop of myself to her. We lay on the stairs for a little while. The only thing that kept us from falling asleep was the desire to drink some more wine. I zipped up. I had her walk ahead of me and kept my hands on her ass, up her dress, and even pulled her down again to kiss her, but she said I'd better not start what I couldn't finish. We poured some wine and turned on some music, and sat outside in the half-warm night. Neither of us ever remembers our conversations: we ask each other questions we have answered several times. She sat on my lap after a while and I pulled down the shoulder of her dress. She was wearing a black silk slip. Are you wearing a slip? I asked. She nodded, as though it were nothing. I began to kiss her again with purpose. Does it turn you on? she asked. I supposed that it did, but I couldn't explain it. I felt her breasts and stomach through the silk as I kissed her. Then she told me to fuck her. Something original. I brought her inside and bent her over the dining-room table, flat, breasts and face flat down, arms out, hands holding the other side of the table, tiptoes gripping the floor, and I pulled the back of her slip up.

I woke, on Sunday, to find her commingled in my white sheets, naked and asleep on her side. The grey blinds in my bedroom are opaque, but around the edges there are apertures where the light cuts through obliquely and violently. Generally, on weekends, I cover my head in pillows, but somehow Clare had them all under her. She also had almost the whole bed to herself. I put my hand on her waist, and she backed into me. I moved her hair away from her neck.

There was no future in it. But the future and I have nothing in common.

18

Dublin is sunbathing. June began yesterday. I have run out of housemates – I am sending Helen texts because it fills the house with her wet black hair – and the clutter is gathering without any reason to tidy it. I do not create disorder; I make room so that it may pass.

7
Satanism

'. . . that thou may'st know
What misery the inabstinence of Eve
Shall bring on men.'
   John Milton, *Paradise Lost, Book XI*

I wrote my first short story at the age of eleven. It was ten pages, longhand, about a group of teenagers on a journey to a cabin in the woods, who are murdered, one by one, gruesomely, by a Satanic cult. I set it on Friday the 13th, and, after some consideration, decided it must also be Halloween. My uncle Troy, a preacher and welder, who went around people's yards rebuking Satan in the name of Jesus Christ and whose wife had visions of Satan at her bedside, typed the story out for me. He owned a machine that was half typewriter, half word processor. He typed all the characters of a sentence, which appeared on a tiny screen, then pressed a button and the globe of the typewheel began to batter ink onto paper. Rendered this way, my story, disappointingly, covered only a single page. Uncle Troy, a short but large man with side-parted black hair, handed it to me as though the event were of such little significance that it did not even deserve reflection. I asked, feeling rather humiliated, if the story was at all scary. Boy, he said – and he squeezed his face together very seriously – I have seen the future, and nothing scares me but the will of God. I did not believe him, and told him so. He said, Let me show you. He opened the bible on the desk – there were bibles all over the house – walked me to the kitchen table, and introduced me to the Book of Revelation.

I come to this imperfect memory – I have no idea how much of it is true; I only broadly know that I am not lying – from two directions: I remember the day for my first short story, and for my first encounter with the Apocalypse. That may sound a little precious. I only mean to say that no matter which path I take back to that anecdote, my recollection of one always leads me to the other.

My mother and I had only just moved to Conroe, following her divorce from my father. In San Antonio, as a Catholic and altar boy, I had drearily studied the Bible and held long and torpid discussions on Jesus with Sunday School teachers. I was intuitively disconnected from Christ. I once told a teacher that even Jesus made mistakes; she corrected me. When we moved to Conroe, I found that people were intensely more religious, or more outwardly religious, but Satan had supplanted Jesus as the central character, and the Apocalypse was more celebrated than the crucifixion. People spoke of Jesus effusively and kindly, but if you let them go on long enough they turned the conversation to Satan. And of all the figures in the drama, Satan was, to me, the most captivating: intuitively he was my man.

It is important to say this: Satan is not an idea in east Texas, nor a myth, nor a figure you must face beyond death, nor a reason not to sin, nor even a metaphor for the capability of wrong and cruelty that exists in the hearts of all men. He is a man who stands in the woods behind your house, or walks your streets, or comes to your bed. Sometimes he wears jeans and cowboy boots, and sometimes he has wings and hooves. I heard of young women who were raped by Satan in the middle of the night – and I met two of them – because they were impure of thought. While Satan, in many cases, was surely a father or stepfather (a stepfather raped one of the girls I knew), in others the experience was purely imaginative or hallucinatory – something from the fever of religion and guilt and loneliness and inadequacy. But there was also something purely wonderful in the thought of it. The stories, which were often passed down by scaremongering adults, turned all of us – at various ages – to impure thoughts. Girls secretly adored him, and formulated rape fantasies. Boys, who were jealous, passed on rumours with pornographic, exaggerative zeal. I still find it pleasurable to visualize Satan with young women. I know it is reprehensible to find sexual gratification in rape, but in my fantasies Satan is always handsome, and the women always want him.

Now and again, my cousins and I filled whole evenings, whole nights, with talk of the Apocalypse. We sat outside in darkness, or in dark rooms, quoting lines from the Book of Revelation, lying about the seven signs beginning. Some said they had seen a red moon, others that a trumpet had howled in the clouds; I told them all that a machine in Switzerland that made credit cards was called the Beast. I am not ashamed to say that I joined rebuking excursions around our houses. Satan had to flee if you rebuked him, but only if your faith was pure. Since ours was not, these excursions were about seeing him. But I think I was alone in the belief, which I dared not share, that if I met Satan, he and I would get along.

I was as fascinated then as I am now with thoughts of annihilation. Beyond the Book of Revelation, I was also obsessed with the certainty of nuclear war. I used to climb on top of the roof of whatever house or trailer home we were living in, and with a pair of old binoculars – my father's – I watched the sky for incoming Soviet ICBMs. I examined vapour trails. My friend Grayson often joined me, and we would say things to each other such as, That is not the vapour trail of an airplane. We would call each other and say we'd spotted mushroom clouds. For many years my mother and I lived in a house whose previous owner had installed a bomb shelter – a large steel tank buried thirty feet deep and connected by a staircase to the living room. But I knew that when war did start, the best place to be was near the blast, so that you were immediately incinerated.

I associate all these things with the manifestation of eroticism, specifically my relationship with masturbation. When I look back on it – the world under threat, Satan haunting the hallways of my house, and the birth of storytelling in me – I see myself and my eroticism as doomed lovers, gathering what beauty we could before it was all over. I know, of course, that there was also something of Orwell's common toad in me: *He goes through a phase of intense sexiness. All he knows, at least if he is a male toad, is that he wants to get his arms around something, and if you offer him a stick, or even a finger, he will cling to it with surprising strength and take a long time to discover that it is not a female toad.*

In some of my nuclear holocaust fantasies – those in which I survived – I was left to wander the smouldering chaos of east Texas alone. I had a motorcycle, and went around siphoning gas from burned-down stations. I had many firearms. I began to find pockets of survivors – including popular girls I knew from school, who threw themselves at me. We fucked around little campfires, often in plain sight of the others – usually her parents. Sometimes I fucked the mothers of my friends while their husbands (often wounded) watched wantonly. I believed the act of masturbation was a sin, and this made me perform the act with more abandon. I masturbated to the fantasy of Satan and me masturbating in a bed together, and once tried (unsuccessfully) to enact this with a friend – with me playing the role of Satan.

One night, at a Baptist church near the interstate – so close you could hear eighteen-wheelers – after the preacher had shouted and frothed and spoken in tongues, and whacked women on the head with an open palm, causing them to collapse and have convulsions on the ground, while the parishioners raised their arms and their eyes rolled back in their heads, I decided to be born again. I believed it was going to be essentially the same as Catholic confession, which I had done on several occasions – though I never confessed anything of substance. The preacher told everyone to bow their heads, and those who wished to be born again should come forward and accept Jesus. I was with my cousin Chris and his mother, Linda, and when I stepped out of the pew, Chris beheld me with derision. Because we never spoke of it, I do not know if he felt I had betrayed an unspoken pact of indifference to this nonsense, or if he, perhaps, had wanted to be born again, and I had stolen a very serious moment from his life. I was guided into a room behind the altar, where men with bibles sat forward on their chairs, waiting for sinners, with the great earnestness of men trying to sell you a deal you cannot afford to pass up. I was not the only person who chose that night to be born again. The little room was full of us, some weeping happily, some quiet. The men with bibles did all the talking. I sat down across from a man with a large moustache and yellow cowboy boots. I didn't want to admit that I masturbated many times a day, sometimes holding pairs of panties stolen from my female cousins, who were older and had large breasts, to my nose and mouth. I didn't want to say that I was *fond* of Satan. But it was nothing like confession. I was told that God knew all my sins and flaws, and loved me nevertheless. I was asked to accept Jesus as my Lord and Saviour. I accepted. The man read some lines from the Bible – none of them from the Book of Revelation – and it was over. He shook my hand. I was reborn. I was sinless, completely and profoundly, for a few hours. The weight was diabolical. Seduction toward another foul revolt is always uncoiling from the tree.

Milton had a true and daring love for Satan. He compares Satan's journey out of Chaos, by perils, to Odysseus's return to Ithaca: *harder beset and more endangered*. I hardly remember studying Homer, in graduate school almost a decade ago, but I see in Milton's Satan much of Achilles and Odysseus: *bie* and *metis*, *kleos* and *nostos*. I am reading *Paradise Lost* for the first time since I was eighteen, when, as a student bound for medicine, I barely paid it any attention. The poem has me thinking of Satan incessantly, admiring him, and is the occasion for my memory of east Texas, and all that came with it. There is something in Milton's love I want to emulate. I want to satisfy my esteem for disobedience, imperfection, eroticism, and failure – not to worship but to fathom, and harness, Satanic *areté*. But I have only a little wrath, which I shall turn inward: I corrupt myself only. This is my definition of love.

The other day, queueing for a cash machine in a cloud of smoke from a burning rubbish bin, I thought of Satan's vanquished army and the Stygian council's debate: Moloch, the sceptred king, advises open war; Belial, the coward, wants ignoble ease; Mammon argues for a free hell, existence to none accountable. Beelzebub, who will propose the corruption of man – Satan's idea – says:

> What sit we then projecting peace and war?
> War hath determined us . . .

Having got my cash, and bought a sandwich and an apple, I had twenty-five minutes of lunch hour left. There were only a few empty spots on benches remaining, and most of them were adjacent to passed-out drunks or fat men with their shirts off. Elsewhere, men and women in suits and sunglasses discussed work. Backpackers read maps and listened to iPods. Single girls read books in one hand by bending the cover all the way back. A group of out-of-work Polish men shared a bottle of something golden. Every man that passed them was asked for a cigarette. A few lovers were out: I picked a spot beside a couple discussing a holiday, but I couldn't make out if they had been on one, or were going. I ate and observed the great lunchtime repose of the city.

That afternoon, we – the reporters – filled the last pages of the issue. I had a small pile of press releases in my inbox and pasted them, slightly rewritten, into the editorial pipe. My way of working had started as a protest: if life was going to deal me monotony, I would deal monotony back, doubled. But my protest went unnoticed. In fact, the editor told me my stories were getting better. Every week we waited so late to lay out pages that our paper was filled with typos. Violent typos. But it was summer, so nobody was reading us.

Adam humbly asks Raphael how and why the earth was created. Raphael has been commissioned by God to lend him knowledge *within bounds*. He reveals that Adam's world is Christ's trophy. And that Christ's glory, great, was scripted. After the battle, Christ, gloating, says to God:

> At least our envious Foe hath failed, who thought
> All like himself rebellious . . .

When Adam asks for knowledge beyond his human status – why create this earth, a grain, an atom, in such disproportion to the firmament and all her numbered stars, that seem to roll spaces incomprehensible? – he is admonished. Milton sends Eve away for this admonishment; she goes to tend her nursery – a miscalculation of her rebelliousness, but deliberate. Raphael tells Adam that the great architect

> Did wisely to conceal, and not divulge,
> His secrets, to be scanned by them who ought
> Rather admire . . .

Why seek to know what is beyond your belief of it? There is plenty on earth to content yourself with. Accept that God's bright luminaries are attentive not to earth but to man. That creation is spacious so that man can know he is not alone. The unknown is on purpose, for your good.

> God, to remove his ways from human sense,
> Placed Heaven from Earth so far, that earthly sight,
> If it presume, might err in things too high,
> And no advantage gain . . .
>
> . . .
>
> Think only what concerns thee and thy being;
> Dream not of other Worlds, what Creatures there
> Live, in what state, condition, or degree –

Adam is cleared of doubt. He is a simpleton – this too Milton makes obvious. (His eloquence, particularly in his plea for a consort, arises from Milton's inability to write poorly.) Adam's mind is made for easiest living, freed from intricacies, liberated from perplexing thoughts. He shall be busy in the prime wisdom: everything that lies before him is his; everything not is fume; it belongs to God.

It is taking me a long time to read *Paradise Lost*: what time I can afford is used as much for contemplation of the poem as for reading it. I allow lines to arrest me. I scribble them on a piece of paper – or whatever is near by – and set aside the book and pace around the house. If it is sunny, I open the blinds and all the windows, and lie on the couch with sunglasses. I wash dishes and do laundry. I eat. I smoke a cigarette. I cannot believe in Adam – I have no sympathy for idiots. I believe in Satan – overconfident, revolutionary, sick of obedience. And tormented: he does not even know why he is sick of obedience. His reasons contradict each other. I watch – in my imagination – his army gathering in the north. Satan was the first hyperborean. Heaven sends a force exactly equal. Michael, prince of celestial armies, fells him on the first day; on the second day they push heaven back. All this is illusion. God has scripted the stalemate for the glory of his Son: He did not mean to quell the rebellion; He meant to make it more worthy of epic poetry. So on the third day Satan, as Hector when Achilles reveals himself outside the walls of Troy, understands that he was never, not for a moment, in control of his fate. Satan was a slave when he was obedient. He remained a slave in rebellion. Christ, grasping ten thousand thunders, knocks the adversary's astonished army nine days out of heaven.

I cannot move on until I have explored the lines within my own memory, until I feel as though I have written them. I cannot help but think of Menard's *Quixote*, and the absurdity of my actions, but everything is autobiography to me, everything – reading especially. To read something is to write it – but I do not recreate the work; I recreate myself. I re-establish the boundaries of the world. All my memories are adjusted, like a man going through a slightly vandalized museum of natural history, repositioning, standing a few displays back on their feet, dusting, polishing.

In February, Evelyn and I went to Riga for a long weekend. I had hoped we'd get snow; instead it misted and rained for three days. Evelyn wore a long white coat with a furry hood. I had a black overcoat. I thought the city would be packed with tourists; it was empty. Everywhere we went, I asked locals where everybody was. They told me it was not unusual.

We got a room in the Europa Hotel Riga, a gigantic space with high ceilings and dark green walls, and views above some unremarkable streets. Evelyn doesn't smile much; there is always a long distance to her gaze. She is the kind of tourist I like to travel with: she is tuned into the eroticism of everything. We dipped into empty bars and kissed; she put her hand down my jeans in a booth; in an alleyway I slipped my hand inside her jeans and put two fingers in her cunt, then let her suck on them. There was nobody around. We had nice meals in empty restaurants. We discussed her fantasies about other women: she wanted a woman to lift her dress up and straddle her face, then let her dress fall down, and in that privacy she would lick and drink the woman's wet cunt. We shared fantasies of her being fucked by other men while I watched, of double penetration, of her kneeling between me and another man, sucking both our dicks. When we came back the first night, she took off everything but her stockings and high heels and said she wanted to be spanked. We moved onto a little couch. She sat on my lap with her back to me, then leaned forward, so that her elbows touched the floor. She put her legs back – her legs are long and fine. She told me she had watched a television show about spanking, and would like to be struck very fast, but not very hard. I did so, and she made the same noise she does when she is being fucked – something between a grunt and a breath. A minute passed, and her ass was bright red on both sides. She asked me to spank her harder; it didn't hurt. I began to, and soon I was battering her: her ass became purple and speckled. Finally I stopped; I could not possibly hit her any harder. She was trembling. Wetness was pouring out of her. I wiped it all over her ass. I put one finger inside her ass and she pushed backwards to drive it in deeply. Then two fingers. I told her I was going to put my entire hand in. She did not answer, but became very relaxed. I got five fingers in. Half my palm. I told her I would push my hand into her stomach. I touched her clit, lightly. She came, I released, and she dropped to the floor like a snake.

I wanted it to be colder: I carried my gloves and hat in my pockets, but I didn't need them. I had a camera with me, a Christmas present from my mother, but Evelyn refused to be photographed, and I had no interest in the buildings. Locals hail Riga as the Paris of the Baltics. I took pictures of some of the Jugendstil apartments on Albert Street – I had heard that it was rather grand – but I found them unremarkable; perhaps I don't know how to appreciate architecture.

On the Sunday we had a few drinks in the Skyline bar at the Reval Hotel Latvia, twenty-six storeys up – austere, straight lines, soft brown-and-violet lights. The city lay in light fog; we were above the fog, looking down on the city, which was grey and black and full of lights. The previous days we had mostly wandered around the Old Town, and it was striking now to see how small it was compared with the rest of the city – we had really seen nothing at all. Evelyn wore comfortable runners, jeans, and a ratty jumper. She drank a few cocktails slowly and read a guidebook to learn something of the places we didn't see. I read the cocktail menu a dozen times, in between long and silent observations of the view. Our flight was much later that night, and there was nothing to do but wait for it, and wish we had another week. I knew then we were doomed to separate – all we had in common was dishonesty and expiring lust – and it was only a question of when, and what boundaries we would cross before it ended. We watched light dwindle out of the sky. From time to time, raindrops spattered the glass, which, in the dimming, grew harder and harder to see through. Soon it was just lights and our reflections. I remember almost nothing of the rest of the evening, except a quiet drive to the airport. Evelyn's eyes were closed. The night was wet. I thought of myself as a boy, on a rooftop with binoculars. What would he make of me in Latvia, in a speeding taxi with a beautiful woman with white skin and black hair? What would he have worried about, if he had known this was the future?

This memory is forever altering. It shape-shifts. It changes colour in the light of my endeavours. Milton must have desired Eve – his verses lust for her; they make love to her. When Satan, within the serpent, spies her alone in the garden, she rapes him – Milton's word – of fierceness, enmity, guile, hate, revenge. This is the immensity of the beauty Milton paints: momentarily she makes Satan stupidly good. Milton owes his own lust to the corruption; he is not the child of Adam and Eve, but of Eve and Satan. We are all in this condition. The image of Eve naked drives Milton to ecstasy. It drives me to ecstasy: that is more precisely what I mean to say. Eve is the force of human rebellion, the desire for equality with the gods. She is Satan's lover. She is the poem.

My memories inform my experience of Milton. The poem also alters my memories. They are studies of each other. They fill each other with mischief, and why not? I begin at a precipice – a memory – and fling myself into the unknown. I like to travel to my mind's exotic destinations, not the places that are easy to reach. I am only happy when I look back and can barely see where I began. The idea of rebirth repulses me; so does remedy.

It is August now. The writing moves slowly; so does the reading. It has not stopped raining for weeks. Manholes are vomiting water back to the streets – they gurgle and spew and overflow – and inundate crossroads and bus lanes. Gardaí in fluorescent yellow jumpsuits direct traffic; sometimes they shake their heads and tell drivers to go back. I think it looks like hell is boiling over, and my appreciation of it confounds my students, who wonder if they're ever going to get a summer.

I carry the poem everywhere with me, and it fills the days with the weight and wonder of corruption, disobedience, and sex. All my thoughts remind me of Eve greedily engorging; of Satan, all impassioned, watching. I see her naked body, dripping, her breasts, her mouth. Her first thoughts are of gratitude to Satan. Her second thoughts are of secrecy from God.

> . . . Heaven is high,
> High, and remote to see from thence distinct
> Each thing on Earth; and other care perhaps
> May have diverted from continual watch
> Our great Forbidder, safe with all his spies
> About him . . .

Next she must decide on Adam. Will she let him partake of full happiness, or

> . . . keep the odds of Knowledge in my power.
> Without Copartner? So to add what wants
> In Female Sex, the more to draw his Love,
> And render me more equal, and perhaps –
> A thing not undesirable – sometime
> Superior; for, inferior, who is free?

Eve returns to Adam, imbecilic cuckold, who, while Eve was off polluting God's creation, wove choice flowers in a garland to adorn her tresses. When she asks him to partake of the fruit, he resigns his manhood; he becomes Eve's subject; he eats,

>   . . . not deceived,
> But fondly overcome with female charm.

Not deceived? But what are the lies he tells himself, that God would not undo creation, since Satan might rejoice:

>   . . . Me first
> He ruined, now Mankind; whom will he next?

The earth, predictably, trembles from her entrails. The original sin is complete. Lust follows, and following lust, shame. God, when he comes to admonish the pair, suggests that Adam is pathetic, that he ought to have given only love, not subjection, to a woman

>   . . . made of thee,
> And for thee, whose perfection far excelled
> Hers in all real dignity . . .

If Adam is a fool and cuckold, then perfection must be flawed. You may argue that Eve was deceived, but the deception is irrelevant. Eve *wanted* knowledge. Anyway, I can see no virtue in innocence. Poetry makes gods of the imperfect. But man is too afraid to live at the pitch of poetry. He creates hell to suppress his hatred of obedience.

    Tomorrow – literally, tomorrow – I will be thirty-four. The number that symbolizes the indomitable victory of Christ over sin and death will pass through me, harmlessly. The city is a paradise of human catastrophe,

Wholesome, and cool, and mild, but with black air
Accompanied; with damps and dreadful gloom –

And I shall stalk it like the figure from my childhood, dragging
the invincible state of failure behind me:

           . . . in this we stand or fall;
And some are fallen, to disobedience fallen,
And so from Heaven to deepest Hell; O fall
From what high state of bliss, into what woe!

Since I see no bliss in heaven, let me live in hell, and eat ash out of
a tree like that which grew in Paradise, and writhe my jaw on soot
and cinder. Grant me strength and daring, that among men the
adversarial in me is most conspicuous; make fire blaze from my
shoulders; urge me to the middle of the fight, where most men
are struggling, and I shall writhe a little, and in writhing, discover.

8

On a Short Stretch of Road in Letterfrack

Art – the stuff a child would call art – does not come multitudinously to me, as they say it does to those who are naturals. I am no good at drawing, or sculpture, or music. I took piano lessons for years and can't play 'Chopsticks'. I cannot dance or sing. The only play I ever starred in, I ruined. I do not even consider myself a natural writer. The more I try not to ape other writers, the less myself I sound. I have an above-average mind, a good attitude toward work in isolation, an appetite for authors who humble me, and I am not afraid of my entrails: that's enough. If I am moved by something, I can put a sentence together nicely; at the very least my style is adequate. I used to measure my writing by its charisma – *such was the way in which at that time I loved my fellow-men; according to the standards of other men* [Augustine] – but now I judge it by its character.

I get my discipline from contempt, from a natural uneasiness; but my inspiration comes from influence. I search for new books, new authors, to uncover more of my nature – some lost strains my habits and prejudices may suppress. I imitate; I repeat; and new selves emerge. Originality is not forged anew; it is borrowed. Originality is a substance in the universe that we pick at, mine for, and give back. My favourites seethe through me. They boil right out of my eyes and ears and fingertips. If literature is a street brawl between the courageous and the banal – that's the way I teach it, anyway – I bring the toughest gang I know: the pure killers, the insane.

The person who reminds me most and least of myself is my cousin Fielding, who is a philosopher – though I am not certain that profession exists anymore. He is about five years younger than me. In all respects, we are entirely similar or exactly opposite. This time one year ago, precisely, he visited from Texas to celebrate the completion of the seven-page essay that took him one year to write. We sat, on a weekday night, at a table in a tapas bar in town, discussing the hope of representing the self; we were, in different ways, attempting that. He hated the transparency of influence in my work. He considered it a sign of intellectual impotence. While undertaking his project, he refused to read anything, lest it seep through. I considered that a sign of pure delusion.

In seven pages, he had set out to tell the story of the evolution of a perfect self, from an infant's first relationship to experience, through all the dehumanizing challenges of life, to a victory for a loving and free consciousness – his answer to the fragmentation and unhappiness in man. He wanted to shine a light for all people. I said I liked it very much, because it seemed to me like a sad and touching autobiography – the story of his failures and his yearnings – and no more. He did not accept this; he had no interest in his own self, but *the* self. Now that he was finished, he would like to make a film of it – I told him I would probably rather not watch it – and then he planned to begin the great project of his life, which was the story of the evolution of consciousness from the first Homo sapiens to the present day.

We ruined the romantic night of a couple beside us. It may have seemed to them impossible that such a conversation could take place. For most of this time I was shrinking into myself, since Fielding had not adjusted to the European volume of speaking. It was only when the guy said something to insult us, not to us but at us, that I joined the conversation with vehemence.

After dinner, we had a few pints – or rather I had pints and Fielding had nothing. He wanted wine, so we went to La Cave. At the time I was living without sleep, and I felt that I was tempting a catastrophic medical condition, and this gave me great, if ephemeral, vitality. I was finally living my philosophy, and this rare predicament demanded loyalty. As much as Fielding had come for his own adventure – he was visiting a friend in Paris the week after – I knew that his father and my father had sent him out of concern for my health.

I begged to know whether or not he liked my writing. He refused to answer: to him the question of liking something was the stuff of an irrational mind. An essay was sound or unsound: it had no other value. He could perform an exegesis, but not a review. I was emotionally battered then, and I nearly wept: I felt sick for caring – my whole premise was that I was past caring. I told him I would quit; I would kill myself. He seemed bored and annoyed by my emotion, and gracefully said he had only wanted a debate, but I was not up for one. We changed the subject, drank the wine and went home. When we got there, Elísabet was finishing her novel on my computer in the dining room. Nothing stopped that woman from creation – she was like some mythic mother figure, birthing new ideas and creatures at the speed of light. I drank some vodka and Fielding had a glass of water, and we all talked for an hour. I felt I might die from frustration.

Fielding's parents always hope I might provide him with some direction when we are together, and as much as he'd been sent to see that I was all right, I also knew his father wanted me to knock some sense into him. The truth is that I felt nothing for his life, and his assuredness, but envy, and I had nothing but admiration for his commitment. He wants nothing in life but to be given space to think, and record his thoughts, and edit them. He is given a small monthly allowance by his father and rents out rooms in a house his father bought for him. He demands absolute silence from his housemates. They are not allowed to play music, and there is no television. He has gone through many phases: athlete, hunter, fiction writer, monk, high-dollar rug salesman. But his most recent incarnation – philosopher – seems to suit him. I studied philosophy as an undergraduate and graduate student – at the University of Texas and the University of Sussex. I also aped as a philosopher. If I read Hegel, I believed and wrote like Hegel. It was the same with Kant, Nietzsche, Spinoza, Schopenhauer, Plato, Wittgenstein, Heidegger, Adorno, Benjamin. In philosophy, I was always a reactionary: at Texas, surrounded by conservative students, I became a Marxist and kept a copy of the *Communist Manifesto* (in German) in my back pocket. When I got to Sussex, everyone was a radical, so I threw myself into American pragmatism and told people I was a libertarian and capitalist.

Since I am not who I am, I must embrace the form that suits me best. Fielding's seven-page essay took him twelve months to write. He was tackling an unimaginably large problem with unimaginable concision. I was finishing my essays as fast as I could type them. He spent a year making sure there was nothing dispensable in his writing, and that nothing was repeated. I repeat myself with recklessness, and since I am the subject, and I am dispensable, there is nothing I say that is essential. He is precise; I am erratic. He refines; I pollute.

I went to the West for a few days after my thirty-fourth birthday. It was the first week of September, and a slow fortnight of teaching before the heavy load of autumn began. I had just learned I was going to be a father – Clare was almost two months pregnant – and there was, and still is (it is October now), a dust cloud in my head from the explosion of that discovery. I have no thoughts that feel right, or if they do, minutes later I'm ashamed of them. I decided I would like to buy a large German sedan, for instance, with an excellent crash rating and leather seats. I decided I would like to live in the country. I decided I wanted another child, maybe another two, with Clare, as soon as possible. She let me discuss these things out loud with myself. And she did not seem too disappointed when I reversed them, only amused. At that time all she could do was sleep and rub her belly: she was starting to put on weight from eating the whole time, but it was good weight and she looked beautiful. Her breasts were large and robust. I groped and sucked them relentlessly.

We stayed just outside Letterfrack, in a white cottage with a red door and skylights in the roof. When we arrived, Clare immediately rearranged the furniture so that the couch was in front of the fire, and fell asleep with a plate of bread in her lap. I felt that I had some job to do, some responsibility. I made sure the fire would blaze. I unpacked the groceries. Nothing else needed to be done. I read from a few of the books I'd brought with me, but I was not in the mood to sit still. I walked outside to take pictures of the landscape with my phone – the inlet, the little road, and Bengooria, the small mountain that stood over us to the east.

The first two days were warm and sunny. This slightly disappointed me: I had hoped for something grey and violent, so that the windows would rattle, and the front door would creak on its hinges, and threaten to blow open – the kind of elements that make you feel that civilization is impossible to reach. Instead I could perch on the fence post outside with a coffee, aim my face into the sun, and watch the traffic go by.

Bengooria is not terrifically imposing – one is never really in its shadow – but it is unique among hills in the vicinity. The English name, Diamond Hill, is fitting: the ground rises up around it, green, tan, rolling, until it shoots up in dramatic grey rock. And when the sun hits it, parts of it go white, so that it could, if you were trying to come up with a name, resemble a dirty crystal. I have a tendency to accept new sights – especially the sublime – as new mythologies in me. The feeling is not exactly articulable; sometimes you feel a thousand years old, sometimes you feel that you are home in an unfamiliar place: it is like remembering, but there is nothing to remember. Sometimes you sense that the earth could tell you stories, that a stone might suddenly shout, You're standing on top of me! or that if you waved a magic wand, all the mountains and trees would reveal themselves as ancient gods and kings and begin to wage war with each other. I did not know what I thought of Bengooria, but it was alone, rather pretty, and exposed, and seemed to draw fascination out of me.

In the stack of books I brought with me, the one I most looked forward to reading was a collection of essays by Tim Robinson, who has spent the past twenty years writing about, and mapping, Connemara. I am tempted, always, to make much of landscape, and to go on about it as though I invented it. But to be here, and considering landscapes, is to be doubly on Robinson's turf. Over the first twenty-four hours, I studied the sight of Bengooria so that I might come up with a word for it, *one bright shining word, small but hard as a stone* [Goyen]. It was on the second day, Thursday, that, reading Robinson, I came across his attempts to name a sight, from the topmost peak of Errisbeg, where *Roundstone Bog becomes visible as a whole for the first time, stretching away to its indeterminate limits, which are often blurred with haze . . .*

> I have tried several times to describe this landscape. Not long ago I went up to look at it again from the top of Errisbeg, trying to find an adjective for it, and the one that came spontaneously to mind was 'frightened'. For a moment I felt I had identified the force that drives the expansion, the self-scattering, of the universe: fear. The outline of each lake bristles with projections, every one of which is itself spiny; they stab at one another blindly. There is a fractal torment energizing the scene, which is even more marked in aerial photographs, in which the lakes seem to fly apart like shrapnel. Of course all this is purely subjective and projective: I was the only frightened element of the situation.

I quote this at length not only because I want to compare his predicament with my own, but because I like it so much. That is all that matters now; I am compelled to write it down again, here and in my thoughts, so that I can appreciate what it might have felt like to write. There was a time in my life when I would not have done so, because I would've been too ashamed not to have done my little mountain more justice than his bog. I might simply have reprocessed the scene and called it my own, or called it inadequate because I was jealous.

There is nothing to be seen in Connemara that Robinson has not studied; no inch of earth he has not hiked across. I know of no project like his – you would struggle to name it. I teach a few of his essays. His mission is, deceptively, a humble one, one that has no glory-seeking: he digs in the earth for stories; he walks; he talks to locals; he has arguments with himself. Like Augustine, he works from awe and modesty.

I do not fear influence; I fear redundancy. In Connemara I keep Robinson's mastery of the place near me. I learn how to observe what he observes. I learn how the landscape wears invisible dimensions: the geological forces, local mythology, the self, the historic. I learn how geography confers consciousness. I try to appreciate death. These things emerge in my mind as one entity, a mood, and if I sit very still I will have it all to myself.

The assumption I always make is that a few days away from the city, without the burden of work, will unleash great productivity in me, or that something I may have struggled with will become illuminated. I feel that I am bound for deep peace. No matter how many times I disprove this theory, I am seduced by it. On the morning of the second day, while Clare slept, I put on some warm and comfortable clothes, set up my computer, made a pot of coffee, and opened a blank page. After twenty minutes, I found myself cutting my toenails. I like to cut an edge and pull slowly across, revealing some of the quick, and when I am done with all ten, I air them out, and press them against the floor. After an hour, with nothing done at all, not a sentence, I was sitting on the floor in a corner, wishing I were dead. A little while later I began – as I do when all hope of writing is lost – hitting myself on the forehead with a closed fist. It is a punishment, but also an attempt to exhaust myself. I have always been like this. The fact that I cannot rid myself of such panic – such vanity – is as distressing as the panic itself, as distressing as the fact that it bothered me that Fielding did not like my essays, even though I proclaimed, in those essays, not to care if they were liked or not. It does me no good, I suppose, to declare that my past is behind me; but I like to think that if I confess, I will be the only one left who believes my own lies. Publicly I have a high opinion of myself. One learns this behaviour – this self-deception – or else one sleeps on the street. But privately I think there is no one more abject, more devious, more insecure, more envious, more desiring of approbation. These are my weaknesses, and in my day-to-day life I conceal them, because I cannot defeat them. I am as much my weaknesses as I am my strengths. But to conceal them here, to myself, would be insanity. So I betray them. I hand them over like spies. I give up their identities. I have them running through the streets of a great dark city. They are chased down blind alleys and assassinated. I do not write because I am honest; I write because I am dishonest.

On the Friday, Clare rose early to leave for a wedding in Westport. I had that day and most of the next to myself, and no car. I could do nothing in the cottage. I read a few more of Robinson's essays, but not deeply. The two dozen books I'd brought, as though I were going away for six months, became a distraction. I had a late lunch. I read and marked some stories by students. I edited something I'd been writing.

The weather, after a sunny and warm Wednesday and Thursday, was slightly melancholy, and the forecast was for heavy wind and rain. If I was ever going to walk up Bengooria, it was then or never, and I had already left it late – Letterfrack National Park closed at five-thirty, and the next day Clare and I were driving to Roundstone, because the Robinson essays I'd read were about that part of Connemara. To get to the hill I had to walk along a narrow, bending road with no hard shoulder, no way to escape traffic, and it was probably the peril of the road that had delayed me. I set out. I brought the essays and stories I was teaching in class the next week – Montaigne's 'On Some Verses of Virgil' and Bruno Schulz's 'The Street of Crocodiles' and 'Cockroaches'. It was about three p.m.

If two cars had come speeding from opposite directions, I would've got squashed. I hurried around bends, and when cars did come, I hopped into the other lane, or jumped on a stone wall overlooking a steep drop, or into a thicket. The wind was already gusting, but the rain hadn't started. Over the sea, to the west, the sky was bright and clear. Behind Bengooria, it was black.

No cars passed, either coming or going, on the long, but not perilous, walk from the main road to the park entrance. I was dressed in jeans and a jacket, and some hiking boots I bought three years ago and had worn once or twice. I wanted to get as high as possible in the short time I had, so I set a brisk pace, and overtook an older, German-speaking couple. I reached the lower summit – to call it this is misleading; it's only a point at which the real hike begins – just before five. There was no way I would get to the top, and anyway, the wind was now shrieking down the mountaintop, and the black clouds were approaching. Rain began to fall. Another group of tourists had reached the lower summit from the opposite direction. They were dressed in waterproof hiking gear, and laughed at me in Italian – I was already getting soaked. I stopped for a moment to gather the view. I remember the sky was still clear above the sea, and the water was like a large flash of light. Behind me, now that I was very close, the rock peak of Bengooria seemed large indeed.

In Letterfrack, at a pub, I had a few pints and seafood chowder. When I go to the West, I only eat seafood chowder: I don't mind that I look like a fool. I also drink Guinness. I embrace the tourist in me. While I sat, I read and annotated the Schulz piece. Schulz wrote the stories in *The Street of Crocodiles* as love letters. I think that is magnificent, and that is how I read them. That is how I shall write stories, if I ever go back to fiction. Then I read the Montaigne, as much as I could before I had to return. I had to leave before it got dark, or I'd be killed on the road for certain. Clare had given me a journal for my birthday, and I filled ten pages of it, copying lines from the essay. Montaigne's humility is infinite. I write his lines not to study or admire, not necessarily, but to tear the last sinews of self-love from my body, to obliterate pretence, to give up ambition. And in that state my own thoughts flow toward nothing, carry nothing of significance, and go where they please.

On the walk back to the cottage, I stepped off the road to a beach of pebble and stone that ran alongside it. It seemed possible that it would bring me most of the way back. It was raining heavily, and nothing of the bright sky was left. I looked behind me: Bengooria was invisible. The water was choppy, swift, swelling. I could not help but think again of imminent fatherhood, but it was not the tide that made me think of it. It was simply the way the world constantly resists man's attempt to make himself profound.

I walked a few hundred metres down the beach. I saw a pier, another few hundred metres in the distance, where I could rejoin the road, but there the tide had come all the way in. There was no way I could scale the wall back. It was too steep and overgrown. I went all the way back to where I had stepped off the road.

9
I Saw a Dead Man on My Lunch Break

Tuesday morning, 14 October
I have been up since four a.m. The more tired I get, the less I want to close my eyes. I dug one of my favourite books out – I have no bookshelves, so I have stacked about two hundred books in seven or eight tall piles in my living room. Clare – who has moved in so we can save money – came up for a bowl of cereal, and each mouthful, to my tired mind, was like a bulldozer scooping up stones. This is someone who weathers my snoring, who is eating food for my child inside her. I feel monstrous for being annoyed. I went outside in the cold and closed the door. I observed my sleepy street – still dark, still waiting for the clocks to change.

Tuesday night, 14 October
Everything I did today was substandard. I drove my Vespa without passion. I wrote the news without the slightest contempt for myself. My little class of top talents, which I finished teaching an hour ago, is bored. I sense that they hate me for boring them.

Wednesday morning, 15 October
I ate two very old bananas, grey on the outside but a little yellow on the inside, still, and drank some coffee. I had a cigarette on the terrace and read from a book a student gave me, Sartre's *What is Literature?* My student has underlined and annotated the book with an energetic seriousness that suggests she thinks she's actually having a conversation. As though she and Sartre are sitting in a café and he is saying these things and she is either nodding contemplatively or waving her hands at him in disgust.

Wednesday afternoon (the office), 15 October
Mary Anne, Nicola and I had a long lunch with wine. It was the first time Mary Anne has spent her lunch hour outside the office since she started ten months ago. Normally she gets soup from the place next door and goes right back to work. We went to a Tex-Mex place near Jervis Street. I ordered a cheeseburger, and the waiter had to run to the shops when I asked for mayonnaise and mustard. The thought of ketchup on a cheeseburger enrages me.

I spent the money I had hoped would get me through the week – starter, main, wine. Nicola wanted to go on drinking through the afternoon; we all did. And for a moment we lived in the thought of that possibility; in that instant we believed our lives had the kind of freedom that mattered, and we saw ourselves crashing down some alleyway at midnight promising never to return to work. But we are back in work. Mary Anne's cheeks have gone purple, and she is swooning under the weight of a headache. Mary Anne has the finest shoe collection I have ever seen – all very high heels, all patent leather. I would like to have her feet in my lap some day. She has a sweet and unassuming face, but the way her heels go maddeningly bam-bam-bam from her desk to the copier makes me imagine her walking on men's testicles.

Thursday night, 16 October
It is almost midnight. I have finished my last class for the week, and I've hurt one student's feelings by telling her I'm sick of her grammatical mistakes, her lack of effort. So I am thinking of her at home, hating me. I'm thinking of every night to come from now until Christmas, of the money I ought not to be spending, of the mortgage. I feel as though I'm in a crowded house, and I've been in it for a year, having long, important semi-conversations over loud music, and people have been dancing on the furniture, but now it has gone a bit sour, and I want to tell everyone the party's finally over, shove them out the door, turn the music off, and sit in a large chair in the darkness.

Friday morning, 17 October
Friday! Catching bus in ten minutes. Drinks tonight with Henrik and Mary Anne. Telling Henrik about the baby.

Saturday midday, 18 October
Up now a few hours. Tired but not hungover. Henrik was happy for me, but for about sixty seconds he was distressed. We were drinking in Neary's, at the table by the door. After saying, This is a surprise, this is definitely a surprise; I'm not going to lie to you; it's a surprise, he said: But if you're happy, I'm happy. Later he told me that, after all the hard living, heavy drinking, womanizing, recklessness, sleeplessness, misery and self-evisceration, impregnating a stable, unselfish civil servant with a PhD, and

being happy about it, might be considered a sell-out. We drank to that. Mary Anne showed up after an hour, having stayed on at the office late as usual. She wore a red dress and fishnet stockings and black high heels – she had worn these things to work. We instantly began a conversation in which I confessed a fetish for patent-leather heels, and a particular fondness for hers that sometimes caused me to stare at her in the office. The comment passed without response, but now I like to think that every morning she may glance a little longer while slipping them on, admiring herself, and know that I am watching out. Perhaps this will create a conversation of gestures between us. Mary Anne looks sophisticated but has the accent of an unsophisticated country woman. She has nice shoulders and gigantic blue eyes.

The Helens arrived – black-haired Helen, who used to dance on my dining-room table and spend all morning washing her hair, and red-haired Helen. It was about nine. Mary Anne went to eat dinner with her boyfriend. The Helens wanted to go somewhere fun where we could smoke. It was chilly – winter is coming along nicely now – so we went to Bruxelles and stood under a heat lamp. The evening had been good. A year ago, I would have been out until four in the morning, but I was yawning and stayed out only because the Helens would have been disgusted if I left before midnight. And I wanted nobody else to show up. Four was enough. A year ago, four would have been a great failure.

I had to sleep upright in bed beside Clare because I had indigestion and, though I had not felt drunk before I lay down, the spins. I woke myself up snoring once or twice. I had a dream that I was on a train, lying down, and watching out the window. City after city went by, Berlin, Paris, Prague, Krakow – I have never been to Krakow – and finally Vienna. It was winter in those cities, and very bright. I saw nothing but buildings and glare. When I woke, I felt as though I had had a vision of the life that has barely escaped me. Not the cities – I can visit any city I like – but the solitude of living in them on my own, and moving on with a suitcase, subsisting but not thriving, working but not saving, slowly falling out of touch with everyone.

Monday morning (early), 20 October
My alarm was set for six a.m., but I woke ten minutes early to the sound of heavy rain. Clare slept through it. For sixty seconds, it sounded like basketballs. Then it was finished. I sat in bed listening to the sound of my heart race – the stress is very bad on Monday mornings. Then the alarm went off, and Clare stirred. She'd had nightmares. It was the movie we watched late last night. I got up and put some clothes on, and have come up to the dining room, and suddenly the sky is clear – still dark above the houses, but orange-pink toward the city. The moon is out, and the light of it is glowing on the wet roof of the building opposite. Low clouds are racing out to the east, away from the city and illumination, toward dawn.

Monday morning (later), 20 October
Got distracted by laundry, and thwarted by an inability to fight through sleepiness. Had to take the dry stuff off the clothes horse, fold it, hang up new wet stuff, take a shower, get dressed, make some coffee, and now I am back, and have spent about ten or fifteen minutes on the web, reading stories that will be out of date by lunchtime. Somehow, in all that, I've lost the guts of an hour.

But I have not eaten – just a cup of strong coffee and a glass of water. I need some toast, or an apple, because if I don't eat I will vomit. But the toast will take another few minutes, and the last apple is rotten. When things are going poorly, and I lose an hour on bullshit, lost time seems like a catastrophe. I am so filled with self-hatred because of it, sitting here now, that I would vomit on top of myself just for punishment – just so I'd lose the rest of the morning having to clean myself up. So I do not eat.

This morning my heart is going rapidly, and I can't take a full breath. It will be like this all day. I hate myself today; I hate the whole human race. I am coursing with rage at the thought of every man and woman alive.

Tuesday afternoon (the office), 21 October
Saw a dead man at lunch today. He had a heart attack on James Joyce Bridge, just outside the Vespa dealership – a little shack on the south quays called Scooter Island, where the mechanics walk around with black hands and black faces, counting cash out of their pockets. The dead man had been walking along the footpath outside Scooter Island, and he wanted to cross to the north quays. He asked for help crossing the road. Mark, the owner, was outside on the telephone and helped him. Mark asked if he was all right. The man collapsed, and a few people knelt beside him and rang an ambulance. While they waited, the man said two names. I didn't hear the names – I had only just arrived – but Mark did. The man continued to speak, but his voice was too weak for anyone to hear him. His mouth made shapes. The ambulance pulled up behind us, and the man died just as the paramedics got to him. Mark was very shaken, and he was talking to everyone, telling his story, inch by inch, exactly how it had happened, pointing to the spot where he first saw the man, where they crossed the road together, where he collapsed, just how quickly the

ambulance arrived, and the last words he said to the man as the paramedics took over. I wanted to be sympathetic, but I had ten minutes left to get back to work, and a fifteen-minute walk, so I wrote a list of problems on a piece of paper – loose steering; back right blinker out; new front tire; engine needs service and cleaning; cutting out – and handed it to him, while he was telling a woman who witnessed it all that the man was trying to tell him something. His head was in his right hand. The phone was in his other. I've never seen anything like that, he told the woman.

Wednesday night, 22 October
Got home tonight at nine-thirty. Did not read on bus. Listened to John Coltrane, and watched the lights of the city go by in my window, and in the reflection of my window. In that moment I could breathe again. Then the lights – the neon Chinese takeout signs, the off-licences, the pubs, the shops, the offices with lights still on – dissolved to the rear, and the bus climbed north, into the suburbs, and I had to change the music, because the landscape had ruined it. I am never content, but I approach contentment through longing, through disappointment.

When the city was behind me, I sent Walter, my cousin in Vienna, a text telling him I had news for him. He wrote back: I am intrigued. Then I sent him a long text explaining that I was going to become a father, and that he would be an uncle. It feels strange to tell anyone that, if only because it is the first ounce of reality in my life.

At home I found a letter from the Arts Council – they are giving me some money to go to Vienna. More money than I have ever received for my writing. I sent Walter another text: And another thing – I'm coming to Vienna in January.

Thursday night, 23 October

I sat down in a café on Baggot Street and opened a book of non-fiction by Saul Bellow. Evelyn had ordered it from the Strand for my birthday, but it had only just arrived. It could have been a year ago – the force of nostalgia was so strong I had to send Evelyn a text saying I was thinking of her. Even though it is over, completely, we communicate once a week or so, often on Saturday or Sunday mornings. I ask her if she got lucky, and she tells me everything. I have no interest in touching her. We have had as much of each other as two people can – we used each other up. But I am still in love with her desire. She watches pornography online and sticks her vibrator in herself for an hour. She sends me texts explaining what she has just done, or is just about to do.

I read from Bellow's essay about Dostoevsky and Paris: that for Dostoevsky the revelation of bias is a step toward truth. That liberalism is inherently deceitful: the principles of good compel us to lie.

Saturday afternoon, 25 October

Clare went to the beautician's yesterday to get waxed. A tall beautiful Polish girl waxed her, with beautiful, soft hands and long fingers. She told me about the experience as I undressed her.

Last year, in the weeks before Christmas, I lived on two hours of sleep a night. I was still teaching, writing, and going to work. In the three months before that, I'd been at the very same thing, if not so condensed – teaching every night of the week, drinking afterward, driving my scooter around drunk and singing songs to myself to stay awake, drinking on Fridays and Saturdays to four or five in the morning, working all day Sunday to get ready for classes. The more fatigue struck at me, the harder I struck back. I bludgeoned exhaustion with drinks and work. I was not trying to kill myself. If I were ever going to lie, that is the one I would tell: that the one truth left on earth is death – that dying is the carnal expression of honesty, a moment of tangible truth. But my onslaught was not a veneration of death. It was a veneration of disillusionment. I pushed myself because I wanted to pour pure poison into my history, kill it, wrench the hypocrisy out. And live with whatever was left, as the most honest man on this earth – I had already been the most dishonest. But an appreciation of death – a real one – is a softer, calmer equation. It is not explosive. It requires deliberation. It is a high, calm fearlessness. It hates all infatuation. And in the face of exhaustion, it tires. It needs sleep.

Tuesday afternoon (the office), 28 October
When I told Evelyn that Clare was pregnant, she cried for five minutes, not heavily, and she did not even know why she was crying. We were in Thomas Read's, the place where we had had our first lunch together and she had given me that book. After five minutes she said she was happy for me.

Tuesday night, 28 October
I came home tonight, instead of going for drinks – even though it was my last Tuesday class – because there was something very definite in my thoughts. A sentence I wanted to get out. But it is almost eleven and I cannot stay awake.

Thursday night, 30 October
The week of teaching is finished. Three more weeks of heavy work, then I coast into Christmas. The chest pains are milder,

and fatigue is starting to have its counter-intuitive effect on me again. The more I am down, the more fiercely I claw myself into existence.

The drive home from work, in the rain, was uneventful, which was a surprise. Last year at this time, Halloween weekend, driving home on a Thursday night, there were large bonfires and drunk teenagers on all the open fields. On the last stretch to the entrance of my estate, the Hole in the Wall Road (a name that tells you what the area used to look like), a bunch of kids ambushed me with bottle rockets. I saw them line up along a fence and light the fuses. The rockets blazed across the road in front of me with blue and orange and green flames coming out of them.

Saturday morning, 1 November
Clare left for China this morning, and there is a palpable emptiness in the house. And in that emptiness, that sudden difference in the pattern of days, I desire to wind this up.

The morning is bright and cold. I have opened the blinds upstairs and am sitting in pure white light. Last weekend the clocks changed, and now I remember the image that started this.

10

Disinformation

It is the beginning of December now. A few weeks ago Clare and I found out our child will be a boy. We went for her twenty-week scan at the Rotunda, and there he was. The woman who performed the scan took measurements and captured photos. She said everything was looking good. I asked if she could tell the sex. She gave me a bit of a lashing: That doesn't matter *to me*, she said; all that matters is the health of the baby. But can you tell? I asked. She sighed, and said it was a boy, then changed the subject. I asked again, about five minutes later, because I did not feel convinced that she was convinced, and she said *yeah* in the way old Irish ladies say it – breathing inward. The doctor later told us that this woman is a bit notorious for whipping men into shape at these scans.

We spent a few days in west Cork to mark the end of my autumn teaching schedule. The B&B we stayed in was mildewy and frigid – the owner turned the heat on for an hour a day only, in the afternoon. I got a cold, and the cold got worse in our damp shivering room. I slept in my clothes, which became damp and smelly, and a winter cap. Clare could not have gone for long walks anyway – she gets breathless quickly – but I had hoped to make a few unexpected roadside stops and wander around some hilltop, and take in the scenery, and think about having a son. Instead, I spent my mornings in a sweaty, hungover, trembling half-sleep, filled the room with snotty tissues, and took so much para-cetamol that, when I finally began to feel better, I had violent indigestion and spent all Sunday and Monday – back in Dublin – lying on the floor between the toilet and the bed.

When Clare and I were leaving – it was a day earlier than we expected, because I was too sick to stay any longer – we took the Caha Pass, in the mountains between Glengarriff and Kenmare. The road goes up and up, high and narrow, and looks over a deep valley of grass and boulders. The sun was out and the sky was yellow. The light was so warm through the window that I cracked it open – and icy air filled the car. At the top of the pass, there is a tunnel cut through the mountain. It is roughly chiselled, not smooth, and the roof drips with condensation. Puddles form on the road. When we came out, and were in Kerry, the sky was black with clouds, and the distances – the valleys and mountains – were clogged with mist. The change was so sudden – the tunnel is only a hundred metres in length – that Clare and I both said *whoa*. A little sunlight from the Cork side of the pass was cours-ing through, and filled the air with rainbows. Nothing is ever striking to me for its own sake; I cannot leave well enough alone. I demand that images like this speak to a self in me that is consis-tent and unvariegated, when in fact it only speaks to the part of me that likes rainbows. I want this sight to wring out of me a feeling that is so big and clumsy that it is almost religious. And when I fail to find the reflection of the image in me, the under-standing of myself in the image, I grow frustrated.

A man does not encounter himself by his secret natures.

Instead, he lives in adulterated memories. He does not know his truth; the mirror in which he gazes upon himself is distorted, too forgiving, and contaminated with bad light. He cannot examine himself: he must first examine the mirror.

For about ten months in 1996 and 1997, I lived in Brighton. My friend Jack, from Mississippi – whom I knew from my year abroad in Germany – was living in London at the time. I was in England to continue my studies as a graduate student at the University of Sussex; he was there to get something exotic on his CV. Brighton was a bore, and I found myself in London almost every weekend. Jack and I were and are very different people. Friends used to say that, while we lived in Germany and were almost never seen separately, we resembled those drama masks: he was always smiling, I was always frowning. Yet we were in love with the same woman, we liked the same authors, and we had the same proclivity toward drink.

I was twenty-two at the time, and so was Jack. His first apartment – about five minutes from the Queensway tube stop – was something like half an attic at the top of a large building, not wide enough for me to lie down in. You could walk from the entrance to the window in four large steps. Jack is about three inches shorter than me, and could just fit on his bed, which was at the window end of the flat, if he bent his knees. But the ceiling was high, and the window overlooking the street was gigantic, and opened to a broad ledge we used to sit on to watch below.

Jack and I picked up the habit of running out on tabs and shoplifting. I stole about fifty books from Foyles bookshop on Charing Cross Road – this was when Foyles was the only bookshop in the developed world without theft detectors. The first time, I stole just one book, *Ubu Rex* by Alfred Jarry. The last time I must have taken five or six. I wandered through the aisles and stuffed them into the waist of my jeans, which was concealed by my coat. In Boots, I'd buy something small and pack twenty pounds' worth of unnecessary items in my pockets. I'd wear three shirts out of department stores. In pubs, if they charged us, we paid, and if they did not, we ran out the door as fast as we could, sprinted until we couldn't breathe, and found another pub.

One day – this was probably spring – we were sitting in Trafalgar Square, up on a plinth beside one of the large bronze lions, drinking cans of cheap beer, listening to a radical religious group tell passers-by they were going to hell. They might have told us the same thing, but we were right behind them, and we were not moving. They wanted to shout outrage at people who wished to escape their wrath, not at people who were, for whatever reason, happy enough to listen. So we drank and yawned and mocked them a bit. Then we stole two bibles from the small stage they had erected. We simply looked those people in the eyes and took the books, as if to say, Try and stop me. A man said, They're free; take as many as you like. But we tucked them inside our coats anyway, and stepped away slowly.

This is how all our Saturdays began: a few drinks in Trafalgar Square, then a wander through the National Gallery. I can't remember why it seemed so funny, but when I dropped my bible in the gallery, Jack said, loudly, You dropped your bible. Moments later, I knocked his out of his hands and said, You dropped your bible. Or maybe that is not how it happened. I can't remember. But I know we began to throw our bibles at each other, across the big rooms, screaming, You dropped your bible! Security began to follow us. When Jack threw his the length of three rooms, we were escorted out. But not before Jack demanded his bible back.

That night, and many other nights, we drank wine and beer at a place called Café Apogee in Leicester Square. It was a large, three-storey restaurant that served drinks until four a.m. We ordered carafes of red wine, and made a big show of ourselves – flirting with our waitress, talking the most enormous shit to each other about art or politics. It was always loud and facetious. We used to play a game in which we argued something viciously, personally attacking each other, but when one of us cried *switch*, we had to change sides, and argue the opposite. When it got late, and the place began to clear out, we ordered the bill and fled. Even after a dozen escapes, some narrow, and even one capture, we were never recognized. We used to enter the place with dread in our intestines, like two trembling cowards leading each other into a dark cave. But when we were not recognized, in that instant, we unwound. Our technique was this: wait until there were other people leaving, walk quietly toward the front door, then bolt. Once, we knocked ourselves down trying to get through the doorway at the same time. We always ran in separate directions, and though we had no idea where the other was going, and had no phones, we always found each other wandering around about twenty minutes later, slightly out of breath. Once, Jack had four bottles of beer inside his coat, and running through Leicester Square, assuming he was being chased, he fell and smashed all the bottles, but was unharmed. I found him trying to hold the bottom of one shattered bottle together, so he could drink the dregs of it.

When he moved to a larger apartment in Crystal Palace, I remember lying around in total stillness, except when we were going places in a panic – always giving ourselves impossible windows to catch the train, eating toasted sandwiches while on the run to the station, which was half a mile away, sprinting with untied shoelaces. Sometimes we made it, and sat in gasping heaps on the way to Victoria Station. Sometimes we didn't, so we drank cans on the platform and blamed each other. We used to start fist fights with each other, waiting for the last bus back from Trafalgar Square – the fastest way to do that was to knock the other's hot dog out of his hands – or throw coins at buses, and run when the drivers came after us.

Of the four or five old friends I have contact with still, Jack's effect on my life was the most tumultuous. When we met in Germany, I was reluctantly studying science to one day study medicine, but my interest was already bottoming out. I nearly failed botany, and passed chemistry only because of a chemical leak in the building during our final exam. I could not understand calculus. I'd taken one or two courses in literature at the University of Texas and liked them very much, but had not done well in them: the cancer of my disinterest in everything else had destroyed my ability to think, or perhaps it was just that I was completely new to a field that required acumen in writing, which I lacked. I had no interest in drinking with the people I knew, in socializing with strangers, only a defeatist obsession with women, and I wrote naïve poems about unrequited love – and that was when I had the energy to act; mostly I stood in my dorm room, looking out my giant window high over the city of Austin, and mourned the premature end of my life. Two years passed – eighteen years old, nineteen years old – and all I had to show for it was the affectation of grief. Then I turned twenty, and moved to Germany for a year as an exchange student, and met Jack, who was studying English literature. From him I learned that good scholarship came from the solidity of language, not the vagueness I had blindly come to adore. It was nice not to feel ashamed of an interest in something like the arts. The acquaintances I had in Austin, until then, would have had a very long laugh if I had said something like, I like the poetry of Dylan Thomas, or (as it was in those early days) I want to walk around the Lake District and read the poetry of Wordsworth.

Jack would sometimes walk over to my tiny room in that German dorm and say things like: I finally get D. H. Lawrence; you've got to live life with your dick in your hands. I was usually watching television at the time: by accident I had become the television broker in the dorm, a position I inherited from the previous television broker, who must have seen something of a Shylock in me. I had a dozen black-and-white sets, and I gave them out for favours and swaps. I gave one for a blow job, another for a David Hasselhoff CD (I could hardly believe such a thing existed), another for a bicycle. I watched incomprehensible drivel – I could barely follow any of it. I wanted to be a writer, not a reader. Jack had no interest in writing, only an appreciation of literature that rounded him out.

I can't remember when it started exactly, but at some point Jack and I began to develop a campaign of repudiation against the kind of society that appreciated things like intelligent conversation. We called this campaign *disinformation*. Truth be told, this was more my baby than Jack's – he was the kind of guy who was everyone's best friend, and inside a hundred different private jokes. But it was nice to have him to bounce ideas off. Disinformation was probably developed while I was in Austin and he in North Carolina – our senior years at separate universities – but

we put it to the test in England. Disinformation had to be prac-
tised to be understood, but we taught ourselves this: you must
come up with an epigrammatic response to every figure, every
theory, every historical event. This response must be dismissive,
both of the actual importance of the subject matter, and, through
that, the unimportance of the man or woman who spoke it – if
it is not dismissive, you do not understand the point of the game.
Moreover, disinformation is a gestalt, a lifestyle: one dismissal
wins you nothing.

This was all incredible childishness, but we lived, that year, by
our faith that every proof of decency was a fraud: the people we
knew pretended to be cultured, pretended to be intelligent,
pretended to be magnanimous, unselfish, successful, humble,
moral, caring. I waged the campaign because I thought it was
funny, and because I was defending my sanity against the things
a postgraduate English student at the University of Sussex heard
during the course of a week in term. One day, our lecturer used
the word *lid* – I can't remember the context. A girl in the class
began to talk about the theoretical significance of the eyelid on
perception and consciousness, and ontology, and soon everyone
in class was debating this: they had lost me (*lost* is inaccurate,
since we were nowhere), but I noted down *eyelid* on my notebook, so that I could come up with a response to it. Finally, the
professor said, That's interesting, but I just meant a lid, like a lid
for a jar. The girl said, Oh, and began to scribble something on
a piece of paper, chuckling away. It should have horrified us all.
Instead, someone proposed that we develop a theory about
eyelids, and give it something like a patent.

I should have walked out of my little house in Brighton with
a backpack and vanished. I would have found some way to

educate myself, live in some tiny flat high above a city street, give up all ambition, and learn a few more languages. Instead, I purged in London on the weekends – enough to go back each week and participate in the conspiracy. Yet I did not just participate, I excelled. I was so adept at drawing together totally incongruous thoughts by theorists and philosophers that it seemed pointless to do anything else.

A Romanian friend has begun to send me her translations of a writer called Nicolae Steinhardt. She seems to have found her stride in it. She says she cannot sleep at night sometimes, and sits at her computer and opens Steinhardt's *The Happiness Diary*, and types a couple of paragraphs, then emails them to me. It is strange to hear of a person translating her mother tongue into her second language, but what she lacks in eloquence, she makes up for with lack of vanity. And a sense of belonging: she has absorbed the book so deeply into her thoughts that she is writing words that belong to her. She lives with her mother and daughter in Castleknock. Her mother does not speak a word of English. Her daughter is a teenager. I like to think of her walking around in the chilly darkness, making something warm to drink, and flipping through her favourite pages by lamplight. *I'm starting to realize that only character matters. Political convictions, philosophical opinions, social origins, religious faith, are nothing more than accidents: only character remains after all the filtrations produced by years of prison – or of life – after all the wear and fatigue.*

Her translations are quiet, sophisticated revolts: they put my time in England to shame. They are acts of adoration first, but also repudiations. I pretend to be doing her a favour by polishing her translations, but the reality is that they invigorate me. Not merely the content, but the image of her at work on them. I think of her awake in her bed, restless. She stands up and puts some slippers on, and a dressing gown. The house is warm and dark, and she does not turn on the lights, because she will wake the others up. She turns her computer on: I imagine there is a window over her desk, which looks out over a street that is busy in the mornings and evenings. She opens a book and begins to translate. Everyone else in the city is sleeping.

II

Abschied

I shall describe my room first. It is a small square with brown-red carpet, brown-gold walls, and threadbare, olive-green curtains. There is a large desk in one corner – the largest thing in the room – which I have already cluttered with books, maps, receipts, toiletries. In another corner is a single bed with a small stool beside it, where I have placed a reading lamp. There is a bookshelf between those corners, but it is already full of my cousin Walter's books. I went through them: lots of self-help material he has collected over the last decade, some religious things. He tells me he has given all that up, but he likes the way books give a room colour. There is a piano on the other side of the room, which I may try to play if I get drunk enough. I am three storeys up, and I overlook the sleepy street – Amalienstrasse, in Ober St Veit, on the far west side of Vienna. There is a small balcony outside the room, but it is too cold to stand on it. Because it is the end of December, the sun is very low, and in the early mornings, if the sky is clear, it burns right through the weak green curtains.

The first time I slept in this room, I was fifteen years old. I was in Austria for a few weeks with my grandmother, Maria. Sometimes, without provocation, the image of my first night

in Vienna springs back to life in daydreams: the picture of Erika
– Herbert's sister – leading me down the short corridor, speaking in a voice so high-pitched that it plays again in my head like
some alarm ringing over a street in panic, referring to the room
as my *chamber* – possibly because she wanted to present me
with some Austrian elegance, choosing *Kammer* over *Zimmer*. I
have not seen the room for eighteen years, and although it was
not a sacrosanct place before I returned to it, somehow it is
now, and I feel as though I have disturbed the grave of a peaceful memory.

The apartment used to belong to Erika, but she lives in a nursing home near Schönbrunn now. The day after I arrived, she had
an accident that knocked all her teeth out – only two of them
were real, but she cannot get new dentures immediately – so she
is too depressed to see anyone outside immediate family. Which
is a pity, because I'd hoped to talk to her about her memories of
Herbert.

Walter has made the old place about as modern as anyone
could without knocking down walls or replacing shelves and
appliances. He has repainted all the rooms – all but mine – in
bold, bright colours. He has also reorganized the space somewhat. The dining room is now a sitting room – and this has
created an unexpected intimacy, a place for long conversations
– and the sitting room is now a dining room with a small space
set aside for meditation and reading, a comfortable chair
surrounded by lots and lots of plants.

The apartment is on the top floor of the building, and Walter's
parents – Dieter and Heidi – live in the apartment below. On the
ground floor is unused office space. Below that is a basement
with a room for big dinners, a storage room – which was, at one

time, Walter's bedroom – and a utility room with a washing machine.

I have six weeks to do nothing in Vienna. Walter is exhausted from December celebrations, and works from three p.m. to five a.m. most days; he's a waiter, and he's just changed jobs. He leaves restaurants much as fickle people leave lovers: the first short while he is overjoyed; then the fighting begins; then he storms out. He seems unable to bear a life without drama – he is gay, yet falls only for heterosexual men – but the drama weighs on him heavily. Every year, usually in October and November, he has a nervous breakdown. He didn't have one this year, and his parents think it's because he kept himself busy renovating his new space.

I travel into town with Walter, we have a beer or coffee, then he goes to work. After that, I go for long walks around the First District to reorient myself. I pause to admire the architecture, even when it is not exceptional. I walk with my eyes up. In the evenings, I observe the city twinkling to life. I am keen to feel something awakening in me, some recognition of myself in Vienna. I visit bars and cafés I remember liking, but do not always enter; I only want to prove to myself that I know where they are. I follow crowds for a while, then abandon them. The last U4 leaves Karlsplatz at twelve-thirty a.m., but I always grow a little restless with solitude, or, rather, faintly out of sorts being seen to be on my own, and head home earlier. I listen to some of Walter's classical CDs – which I've begun to copy onto my computer, so that I may transfer them to my iPod and play them while strolling through the city – and drink two bottles of wine, finish my pack of cigarettes, and fall asleep.

The amount of space the city inhabits in my mind is totally

out of proportion to the time I have spent in it. I came for a few weeks in 1990, but travelled a good deal elsewhere in Austria. When I lived in Germany, in 1994 and 1995, I came to visit three or four times, but never for more than a handful of days. In 2002, I spent one month here. In 2005, a week; in March 2008, five days. That is all – no more than three months altogether. But when anyone asks, I tell them I have lived here an incontiguous year, at least.

I was once very close to fluency in German – so close I could fake fluency – and the language comes back to life in me, slowly. I have already had long conversations with Walter, and separately with Dieter and Heidi, and on the telephone with a friend, Christl. Talking stirs the language out of dormancy – there is no other way for me to remember it. I begin a sentence like a man jumping from an airplane without checking his parachute. I arrive at the spot for the word, and suddenly, the word has come out of my mouth, and the sentence drifts coherently to the ground. Or the word does not come, and I must approach the subject from another direction. German words storm my inner English monologues – *mühsam, leider, leisten, unerträglich, Ausnahmen, undsoweiter. In the beginning*, I might say, when I speak to Clare on the phone, because my brain is getting used to starting sentences with *Am Anfang*.

I like to memorize interesting words from books I really ought to be reading in English. This time I have brought along Wittgenstein's *Philosophische Untersuchungen*. I jot down nice words in a large spiral notebook I brought from Ireland – this morning it was *irreleitend* (misleading) – and spend the day inventing contexts to use them in. The first time someone hears a foreigner with bad German use *vorführen* correctly in a sentence, they are astounded; the fifth time in an hour, they grow suspicious. All this means I am confounding people with advanced speech, or idiom, or accent, one minute, and idiotic mistakes, or baffled simplicity, the next. The other night, Walter asked me to explain some of Wittgenstein's concepts. I handled this with some fluency. But when he asked me what I did on New Year's Eve – he had to work, so I spent the night with family friends – I was stumped. I simply said it was lovely (*genial*) but extremely cold (*abarschkalt*) – we spent the night drinking on the street, listening to music at various points around the inner city – and that I was tired and had a headache. I have no flexibility in German; I lack the capacity, so far, to rearrange what I know into something that is individual, original. I think this must be exactly how a small child approaches language: when he imitates, he succeeds, but he cannot express himself through imitation; he wears the language like ill-fitting clothes.

This morning – Saturday, January 3rd – I was awoken by the sound of something scraping the street. People who are used to cold climates will think I am an idiot for not knowing immediately what this was. It had a burping diesel engine, and it came down the road slowly, twice. On the first occasion, it woke me, and I checked my phone for the time: it was not yet six. The sky was still dark, and the light in the street was blue – above the front door of our building there is a blue, illuminated sign for the office that is no longer open. I tried to go back to sleep. About half an hour later, the sound returned. It was extremely loud. I turned my light on and picked up Wittgenstein, but I was too tired to make the effort. The noise became so potent, so close, that I got up to investigate. I opened the curtains and looked out: the street was still glowing blue, and the sky was dark, but I could see that it had snowed during the night. The rooftops across the street were white, and the plants on the window sills, and all the parked cars. I stepped onto the balcony. I had nothing on but boxers and a T-shirt. I tiptoed: the stone surface was like ice. I leaned over the edge and saw that the vehicle – a snow plough – had cleared a narrow black path down the middle of the street.

I stayed outside a moment longer, arms crossed, bouncing slightly. I had the morning all to myself, it seemed. It would be hours before the city woke up. When I went back inside I put my headphones on and listened to some music Walter had recommended – Saint-Saëns. I lay in bed looking out the window, thinking of the day that was to come.

Walter had last night off work. He has worked every other night this week until five a.m. He is forty-two now, and he's been waiting tables since he was nineteen. His new restaurant has two *Hauben* – a *Haube* is a kind of Austrian Michelin star – so he makes a lot in tips. Yesterday he slept until two, and we hung around the house until late afternoon; it was already dark when we arrived in the First District. I bought tickets for a concert at the Musikverein. Then, at his restaurant, we bought some nice wine for a dinner party his friend Wolfgang was throwing later that night. A few of his colleagues were drinking espressos and smoking cigarettes at the bar. The girls were wearing tight white button-down shirts and black trousers, and they had that air of high indifference one associates with waitstaff at a fancy restaurant. I wanted to introduce myself, but I was suddenly very ashamed at the state of my German, and hung back.

We had a few drinks in Loos Bar – a little place designed by

Adolf Loos in 1908. It seats about ten people, and another ten can stand at the bar. When I was here in 2002, I drank there almost every night. Sometimes we would go for a midday pick-me-up, then back in for the evening, or start the evening there and pop back in at three or four for a nightcap. Last night, Walter drank two vodka gimlets and was tipsy. He'd had nothing to eat since waking up. I always know when he starts to get drunk, because he speaks English, or German with an American accent. He told me that to celebrate New Year's Eve he gave a patron a blow job in the bathroom of his restaurant. He simply walked into the bathroom, saw a man having a piss in a stall, with the door open, and joined him. An hour later, the man left with his wife.

Walter has not had a homosexual boyfriend since 1992, when he lived for a few months in Texas. This sounds a little strange, but in Vienna there seem to be many straight men who experiment with other men – particularly macho Turkish men, says Walter. I believe he nurtures disenchantment in the same way that he takes care of the plants in his apartment, or the back garden in summer: he dusts them, mists them with a bottle, speaks to them, and maintains them in perfect condition.

He has started to dress conservatively in middle age – unripped jeans and ironed, long-sleeve button-down shirts. So when we are both dressed to go out, we look somewhat similar, except that he is a little shorter, and made of nothing but skin and bones: at five foot eleven, he weighs only sixty kilograms. He tends to skip breakfast – he is usually asleep – smokes cigarettes for lunch, works without food, and picks at ham and cheese when he gets home.

Walter is the only great-grandson of Octavian Augustus Fuchs – Herbert and Erika's father – who does not look uncannily like

Octavian: he looks like his mother, Heidi, and he is the only male descendant of Octavian who still has his hair. Of Octavian I know very little, only that he was a disciplinarian who, in his twenties, was a member of an exclusive club where the initiation rite was to be cut open with a sabre from the ear to the lip; then one stitched oneself up, so the scar would be coarse and jagged.

But even with the head of hair, Walter looks older than he is. This is the effect of twenty-five years of heavy drinking and ciga-rettes, and twenty years of drugs – daily use. I have seen pictures of him as a teenager, when he was angelic, but even then his eyes say he is going to live without happiness. No matter how many faces there are in a photograph, his eyes are the ones that attract your attention.

I had a coffee at a café near the entrance of the Hofburg. I sent Clare a text saying I was bored, which was unfair, considering I had left her on her own and gone in search of adventure, but she wrote back to say that I should find some pretty American students to play with. I liked the idea, except I caught a glimpse of myself in a window: alone, and with nothing to do again, I looked a bit sinister.

I left the café and booked a room for myself and Clare – she is coming for a few days shortly – and then had a drink in Santo Spirito, my favourite bar in the city. Santo Spirito is an old, out-of-the-way wine bar on the Kumpfgasse, not far from St Stephen's Cathedral, that plays nothing but loud classical music. If you request Wagner, you are thrown out – this is what Walter told me, and the bartender confirmed it. It was empty because it had just opened for the evening, and I had a few glasses of wine while trying to improve my German with Wittgenstein. I considered the sad fact that Wittgenstein, a philosopher I struggle to understand in English, was my only companion in the city. I was too ashamed to send anyone a text telling them I had come all this way to feel sorry for myself, so I packed up, hopped into a nearby restaurant for a cheap schnitzel, and was home before nine. I opened a bottle of wine and made some spaghetti Bolognese for Walter, in the hope that pasta might fatten him up a little, and listened to some more of Walter's music – Bruckner.

Today is Sunday, and Walter is drinking with colleagues at their Christmas party, which will go on all night. It snowed in sunshine all day, which was beautiful, since I had never seen anything like it, but I didn't leave the apartment. Dieter and Heidi are away today, so for a few hours I played music so loud it could be heard up and down the street – I had cracked two windows to let in fresh air – and sat very still on the couch. I turned the music off briefly to watch ski jumping on television from Innsbruck. Now it is night.

After a very forgettable guided tour of the city – I wanted something different to do, and a refresher course on Viennese trivia – I decided to buy a book in German that was not Wittgenstein. I went into a bookshop near the Stephansdom and told a girl who worked there I was looking for a great book by any Austrian author, and she recommended Peter Handke. This is like giving an Austrian man, with bad English, a copy of *Ulysses*. So now I have a book I can barely make sense of, and I am reading it in Viennese cafés, having no idea whether I like it or not, since I have only bursts of understanding. I suppose I could read newspapers, or children's books, if improving the language were really that important to me. But I don't want to read newspapers, and

I am too impatient for simple books. There was a time I could have made enough sense of Handke to translate him. I flip the pages anyway, so that I look like I'm making progress.

I had plans to take another tour, but by the time I got to town I had lost the desire. I only wanted to travel around in streetcars and walk the streets, and maybe get my head shaved – Walter says it is a good idea, and sympathetically adds that it would not look much different.

Café Diglas: a seat in a booth at the back. The Viennese are eating cakes. I have the best view in the place, staring down the long row of packed tables. White tabletops without tablecloths, luxurious red chairs, large and delicate chandeliers. There are two Viennese women in the booth next to me. They are speaking too fast for me to make sense of anything, so I observe their mouths, their tongues. I would like to lean over their table and be licked by them. I want to spend the afternoon rolling around in their breasts. I think about the shape of Clare now, six months pregnant, and I have a raging desire to pull my dick out and politely ask the women to feast on it. Cakes arrive, and they accept them routinely, without breaking the conversation, merely moving their arms out of the way so that the waiter may place the cakes gently on the table. And the women begin to eat between sentences. I request the bill and begin to pack up. The café has assumed a rapidity all of a sudden, and everyone seems to be departing. It is inexplicable, but I decide to be part of it.

A long walk behind the Rathaus, up Florianigasse, into the Eighth District, then a right, in search of Laudongasse – the memory of 2002. I find it, but it is emptier than I remember. I have my headphones playing very loudly now – I am giving Mozart a chance, even though he is somehow too perfect for me, a perfection so clean and alien that it seems to have no personality. Yet the violins are going; they are tearing open little fissures in the universe. It is like watching a great battle from a long distance, and very high up; whereas someone like Tchaikovsky puts you in the trenches, with bayonets in your neck. I catch the number 5 because I see two black-haired teenage girls hop on – they are both in black jackets and dark blue jeans. I stand so close to them that I can smell the shampoo in their hair. We all jingle-jangle up the road, with the deep clang of the streetcar bell and the little automated voice telling us what the next stop is, and if there are connections. The girls get off somewhere, but I stay on until Café Hummel. I sit down for a bite to eat and a Melange. In March 2008, Walter and I drove up to a spot in the hills outside the city, where there is a stone circle, and where the beginning of spring is celebrated with bonfires and Bach's *St Matthew Passion* on loudspeakers. There was a full moon, or nearly, over the city that night, glowing yellow-white. Now I am watching streetcars go by – the 33, the 5, the 2. There is nothing at all to this connection, but somehow the two moments link, they move by each other on the street like the 5 going toward Westbahnhof and the 33 heading back to Laudongasse.

Walter and I went to the Konzerthaus to hear the Budapest Festival Orchestra play Brahms and Prokofiev. The tickets cost twelve euro each: our seats were nosebleeds. I nearly fell asleep during the first Brahms piece; it was nondescript, and I was very tired. I was also dehydrated, and my throat was sore, so I kept clearing my throat. The woman in front of me turned her head every time I made a noise, and I felt so enraged by this that I slammed my knee against her seat every time she turned her head. The second piece was Prokofiev's second violin concerto, and a beautiful Japanese woman in a glittery silver dress – the soloist – woke me up. I also preferred the Prokofiev. *Preferred* is inadequate. I felt rather shocked by it. It was erratic, impulsive, imperfect. But I am not qualified to discuss music. I am merely equipped with ears. I watch the world-class musician with the same bewilderment that a caveman might feel after getting struck down by an automobile. The concert played on – another, much better, Brahms piece – and Walter began to perform little head bops at all the big moments. He began to conduct very subtly with his fingers. The musicians were bouncing in their chairs. They attacked their own noise. The conductor leaped and beat at the air. The concert house was suddenly thick with sound. I felt that if I stuck my tongue out, the sound might taste of gunpowder. And then it ended. The orchestra played a raucous Hungarian dance by Brahms for the encore, and we stormed the cloakrooms, a thousand of us, all at once, and filed out into the blue, icy night. A man with a violin case went by us in a dirty overcoat. He was shaggy, and it seemed to me that there was ice on his beard. I loved the sight of him. To me he was the last genius on earth. I imagined that he had played in the fourth or fifth row of some philharmonic, maybe twenty years ago, and quit in order to compose something new, a last symphony, a symphony that would murder music forever. And I imagined that he had not written a note of it yet.

Clare arrived for a long romantic weekend, and has now gone. The city has grown exponentially colder. My skin is so dry that I am scratching it off myself. My elbows, thighs, calves and waist have long claw marks that bleed: I wake myself up in the night scratching. Walter's love life has become rather tumultuous and full of possibility, and as a result of that and a dozen other things – his work schedule, his drug habit, his belief that he has stopped existing, or has not existed for twenty years – he has developed a very bad pain in his neck, and goes around the house like a crippled hunchback. He is taking medication and gets massages from his mother, who was a nurse. The sight of Walter in pain tends to bring everyone around him down, not because he complains but because he becomes so disappointed in himself. And you cannot help but feel that you have somehow contributed. Today – a sunshiny Monday, with snow glowing on rooftops – he can barely walk. I saw him boiling the kettle for a hot-water bottle, and while he was waiting he began to collapse slowly – his knees could not take the weight – and only stood half-upright again when I appeared behind him to ask if I could help.

In 2002, when I spent four weeks in Vienna, I made very good friends with a woman named Onka, a beautiful, large-breasted restaurant owner ten years older than me, half Swedish, half Austrian. She is, now, in an unhappy relationship, Walter tells me, and she has not returned the call I made to her. During that visit, I spent almost every waking hour with Walter (who was unemployed) or Onka, or both – and Walter's brother Michael was often around, and a band of A-list gay men who wrote and starred in cabaret and drag shows. I am thinking of Lucy McEvil in particular, Austria's most famous drag queen, who lives in the hills outside Vienna, in a house she calls Villa Valium: she has nothing but vodka in the house, and a few fine foods to nibble on.

Michael, in 2002, was single and overlascivious. He used to stroke slim glasses of drink in crowded bars and moan and whimper, and accelerate until he came. Sometimes he did this in the middle of the day, in cafés, with children around. You never saw anything like it, him wiping his brow afterward, and a child staring at him in horror. Now he is in a stable, exclusive, and very sweet relationship with a young eastern European man. He does not go out anymore, and I have only seen him once since I arrived. I asked Walter if he wants the same thing – a kind of marriage, even something that allows for sex with other people. We were at the bar up the road from the apartment in Ober St Veit. It was empty except for me, Walter, and the voluminous blonde barmaid, who has a mole on her upper lip. All our nights out together, this time, seem to take place in this empty bar. The worst music imaginable is played there. He could not really answer the question. All the answers are easy to say, but none of them are true, he said.

Yesterday I bought a little Moleskine notebook – incredibly over-priced, but small enough to carry in my pocket. I was sick of carrying a bag around with the old notebook, and I'd started writing German words I wanted to remember on my hand. With Clare away, I was spending time with Wittgenstein again. I try to memorize my favourite words in his book, but it will be difficult to put them to use without forcing them into unlikely contexts. My list includes words like *unwägbar* (imponderable), *willkürlich* (arbitrary), *mannigfaltig* (variegated), *die Öde* (barren-ness), *beunruhigen* (to trouble), *das Bestehen* (existence), *bildlich* (figurative), *die Täuschung* (illusion), and *isoliert* (isolated). I haunt the little alleyways of the First District coming up with sentences to use these words in – words that choose me, and *nicht das Umgekehrte* (not the other way around). The cold loosens its grip a little, and I turn down the collars of my pea coat and take my gloves off. The language absorbs my identity into it; somehow I solidify into the form that is the imponderable calculation of relationships of meaning and use, and the past, and of memory. And the more solid I become with language, the more imponderable I am.

Reading the section in Wittgenstein on his association of *fat* with Wednesday and *thin* with Tuesday, I realized that I associate all my memories of Vienna with the colour blue. In fact, I have painted blue into my description of the city, even when it does not exist. The light outside my window, for example, is absolutely white; I imagined the blue. Yet without the association, the memory is ungraspable. No other colour works. If I think *green* at the same time I think *Vienna*, I can think of specific green things: the roofs of some buildings, especially the Jugendstil underground stations, or the gardens I have visited. But if I think *blue*, my mind floods over the image of the city all at once – main streets and alleyways, tall buildings in fog, music, packed night-clubs, Walter, drag shows, Onka, eating Käsekrainer on the street.

I have discovered that if you want to see the most beautiful women in Vienna – and there are beautiful women everywhere – one thing to do is take the U4 from Schwedenplatz to Hietzing at rush hour. There are probably a handful of other stretches of underground they move in, but this one is the one I know. I put my headphones on and blast my new Prokofiev – for instance – and stand at one end of a railcar, and look upon them. This is prurience, but also, and more so, awe, admiration, pain. Then I come home and cook Walter some dinner, so he can relax and recuperate. He is deteriorating, and never smiles. Some nights I return to the city, and some nights I stay in and listen to music – there are very few CDs left to copy.

Living in a kind of interdependence with Walter, recording my days as if they mattered, going to concerts in the cheap seats, smoking two packs of cigarettes a day, drinking anonymously, slowly assembling an identity in German – my time here is an imperfect glance at a life I will never know. My time here dissipates. It seeps through a drain. The thought of work again, of small-mindedness, of the manufactured emergency of news – I don't know how I am supposed to go back to that. When Clare was here, on the first night, she began to describe the state of mind at home, the panic of financial meltdown, loss of jobs everywhere, how dismal and unhappy life had become. It had been more than three weeks since I'd read a single line of news about Ireland, or anywhere else, and I had to ask her to stop. She wanted to stop, she said she could not bear to go on about it, but the news had its teeth in her. Few people really understand how the news is made; if they did, they would never pick up a newspaper again. After four days here, everything that she had worried about seemed less important than the act of eating a nice breakfast, or a night out at the symphony.

I quit Wittgenstein for a while and bought Henry Miller in German – *Der Wendekreis des Krebses*, a title not quite as romantic as *Tropic of Cancer*. I have read the book enough times to understand the gist, even when the words are out of reach. Walter also has a copy of the book in English, which I gave him in 2002, to mark our time here. I read and write down words I know I want to know: *Ungeheuer* (monster), *Unflat* (squalor), *krumm* (lopsided), *uneben* (uneven), *blinzeln* (blink), and *Dirnen* (trollops). Miller somehow does not suit Vienna. Wittgenstein is blue; Miller is another colour. The words in Wittgenstein have a diminishing effect on me, a vanishing effect. Miller electrifies. He vomits. Then there is Handke, who suffers, who hates Austria. I try to let each vocabulary exist at the same pitch, and interweave them, so that I am always disappearing and trembling and desiring and suffering and hating. I accumulate the language of essence only. Yet all this has started to bore me, since I feel that existing in this way is something I have already accomplished, and may not be an end. I have grown weary with the weight of language, and it only makes me more of myself. The only thing that seems different now – different enough to justify so many weeks in Vienna – is my interest in music, which I play not as background noise while I read or eat or tidy up my room, but without distraction, loudly, as loudly as Walter's speakers will play it, sitting very still, or lying down, or on my headphones in the city: I am perfecting the art of strolling around, watching the city unfold by alleyways, the slow and rolling film of altering perspective – to music; music that suits this city more than any other.

The book is finished. This is just an exhale, a lingering glance, an experiment in superfluousness. I have always dreamed of a book with a last chapter that was unnecessary, that went on too long, that took place somewhere else, with other people, and left the old story to flap about in the breeze. I am not in search of a self. I am leaving one behind. I plan to cast the self who came here into oblivion – the author of this book, who has nothing more to say. I leave it here, in the cold, in this record, which is the sum of my experiences in the city, so that it may prowl around as long as it likes, sit and talk with Walter in his apartment for eternity. This morning I woke a little later than usual. Walter had gone to his physiotherapy. I washed the dishes that were left over from the night before and turned on some music – Maria Callas singing Verdi, Puccini, Rossini. I took a bath – I have not mentioned that I am starting to take baths now. I made a cup of green tea, which helps settle my stomach, and sat in the living room for a very long time, without movement, and watched the smoke from my cigarette settle in the still air of the room. The self I shall leave behind will be doing this forever.

The desk in my room has become cluttered with remembrances – programmes from concerts, exhibits, receipts, unfolded clothes, and my books: I have now officially given up reading, and I feel reborn because of it. Dieter and Heidi gave me a picture of Herbert, which I have leaned against one of the twenty potted plants. Our eyes are still alike – according to Clare – but the uncanny similarity has vanished. My face has broadened a little and I look like Octavian now – though who knows what Herbert would have looked like if he had reached my age? I have also learned that he did not die in Carinthia, as I remembered Maria telling me, but in Southern Tyrol, which is now a part of Italy. I can't sleep late: the mornings have been sunny recently, and the light ignites the room, and slowly I begin to boil under the duvet. I throw it off. I lie on my back, play music, and stare at the haze – the absolute stillness of everything. If there is any water left in my glass, I finish it. I check the time on my phone. It is always earlier than I wish.

The other evening, I met an old friend named Michi. He's a politician – a socialist – in Wiener Neustadt, a little town about forty-five minutes by train to the south. We first met in 1995, when I was living in Germany. He was the boyfriend of an Austrian girl I knew from Texas. He spent a few days showing me around, talking about the possibility of a just and equitable society, and denouncing greed and unnecessary wealth. He is very small, which somehow suits the intensity with which he speaks about injustice. We met again in 2002, and I spent a night with him and a bunch of historians, politicians and intellectuals in Wiener Neustadt. I remember a room full of wild hair and huge beards dripping with beer suds. At the time he was starting his own publishing house, a non-profit venture that would publish books nobody else would – local history, political dissertations, and so on. It is flourishing now, and he, alone, has written something like a dozen books for it. They never make any money, and everyone works for free.

We met in Café Westend, which is at the top of the Innere Mariahilferstrasse, and would have had a view of the city's main train station, Westbahnhof, if it weren't concealed in a building site. The café was large, pleasantly run-down, and sparely decorated. Michi waved from his booth. He wears nothing but black – black trousers, black shoes, black shirt, and black suit jacket, even in summer. I had forgotten that, and I felt a little stupid in my blue shirt, jeans, and hiking boots. We shook hands and sat down and he ordered me a beer. His life had gone largely unchanged since we last saw one another, except that he had married his long-term girlfriend, so I spent the first half-hour catching him up on mine. He scratched his head afterwards. Crazy, he said.

Michi is thirty-eight, and now that his party is in the ruling coalition he has hope that things will change for the better. I wonder at his determinedness – politically I have none at all. In another bar, a little while later, over a plate of chicken schnitzel, I told him that I never had my own political position on anything, except contempt. He said that is a type of politics. I disagree, but I knew what he meant. I did not have the German to keep up with him. And anyway, I knew that arguing would prove his point. I proved mine, or tried to, by telling him he was right.

Walter does everything with a cigarette in his mouth, it seems, and a cup of coffee or tea near by, and he is usually a little drunk and stoned before noon, though he conceals his morning drinking. He's off work now, because of his neck. This morning we watched the downhill skiing. Austria finished second and third, and Switzerland was victorious. Oh well, he said, the slalom is tomorrow.

He proposed a *Spaziergang* – a hike to get some fresh air and exercise, and of course to get a view of the city from high up. This is a hike we seem to make every time I'm in Vienna, except that this time much of the trail to the top was ice, so after a chest-incinerating ascent through the wealthy streets of Ober St Veit we had to claw our way, branch by branch, up the steep slopes through the forest. Since the woods are not evergreen, you could see limitlessly through them, thin brown trunks and leafless branches, and the sunlight blazed crisply off the icy earth. When we got to the top, Walter smoked a cigarette and we tried to identify different churches in the distance. The air was almost white. In the summer, Walter and his parents rent a little bit of land on the hillside to grow vegetables. Many small plots are for rent. He tells me, as we walk beside the spot, which was all ice and sludge, that on nice days in June, July and August, there are dozens of people digging around and tending and gathering. Walter says he wants to move to the countryside and do nothing but work on his garden, to have his elbows in the earth. I ask him if he'd miss anything in the city – the sauna, perhaps, though he can live without sex for long stretches, and concerts, and the shrimp dish at Umar Fisch.

I cooked enchiladas that afternoon for Walter and his friend Martin, a hairdresser. Martin had been out until six a.m. the previous night, and had two hours of sleep before going to work. He looked as though vampires had been feasting on him for a week. He ate with his face an inch away from the plate. After his last bite, he stood up, walked to the bedroom, and did not return. Walter was heading into town with his friend Carolin for a piano concert in the Musikverein: Beethoven, Scriabin, Prokofiev, Chopin – and Carolin was supposedly friends with the pianist, and everyone was heading to a restaurant in the Eighth for a post-concert party. Walter wore a very conservative black suit, white shirt, and red tie. He said he needed the red because all the colour had seeped out of his face.

I took a nap, and when I woke up, Martin was sitting on the couch across from me, watching a blank television screen. I poured myself a glass of wine – I didn't want to show up to the party cold sober – and Martin gave me a haircut. He clipped it without a guard, and afterward I was shocked at the sight of myself. It had never been so short. It was, effectively, gone. Do I look like a neo-Nazi? I asked. Lazily he said anything is better than being bald and letting your hair grow – he is bald also. Then he went back to sleep. After an hour of staring at myself in the mirror, I grew a little more accustomed to the sight.

I took the U4 to Pilgramgasse and the 13A bus to Laudongasse – if I had stepped off the bus and walked ten feet further, I'd have seen the restaurant that Onka owns. But now that Onka seemed not to want to see me, for whatever reason, I didn't want to do damage to my memory of the place, or of her. I stepped into

Dionysus, the restaurant where the party was being held, and I expected a great deal of commotion – the pianist surrounded by young women, the owner delivering bottles of champagne to every table, scandal, quarrels. Perhaps even some singalong tunes played on an old piano. If I were a concert pianist who could sell out the Musikverein, I'd have expected nothing less. Instead, one half of the restaurant was empty. Walter was at the bar by himself smoking a cigarette, because he and Carolin were at a non-smoking table. Seeing Walter smoking by himself in a conservative suit in an empty restaurant on a Saturday night made me very unhappy. The pianist was not there, he said. Maybe he would come later. Carolin and I said hello – we had met briefly the previous March – and we sat down with a handful of dreadfully boring people who refused to talk to us. I asked them if they had liked the concert and they said it was nice, and then went back to each other. I looked at Walter and he shrugged. I have no idea who they are, he said. Carolin explained, but I wasn't listening. I was trying to get the attention of a blonde waitress with a beautifully long, crooked nose, so I could start drinking.

By midnight Walter was yawning, and we decided to get our coats and have a drink somewhere else. I put on my coat and stood at the bar and smoked a cigarette with Walter, while Carolin and the owner – a Kurd – chatted about the smoking ban. He said it was a good idea, since he didn't smoke – except that he was chain-smoking. Nobody made anything of this. We were on our way out when Carolin's eyes opened very widely and she shouted, Maestro! I turned to see the pianist arrive. A corner of the restaurant stood up to applaud and shriek praise. I was closest to the door, and inexplicably he stuck his hand out at me. I shook it. *Servus*, Carolin, he said. Carolin tried to get to him, perhaps to kiss his hands, but he was already moving to the table that was applauding him.

I woke late on the Sunday, and Walter called Lucy McEvil to see if we could have some coffee at Villa Valium. She said to come by anytime – on weekends she was performing on stage in a very camp version of *Lady Windermere's Fan*, but during the week she mainly wrote and composed and worked in her garden.

We walked. It takes about thirty minutes to hike up to her place in Baumgarten, in Hütteldorf. She was outside in the garden when we arrived, holding a little spade and an axe. Lucy's real name is Martin, though nobody but the bank refers to her as Martin. She is very tall with long arms, long legs and long fingers. She moves very slowly and sweepingly. She is not a transvestite – she is an entertainer. Outside of entertaining, she dresses like a man. But everyone still calls her Lucy, and still refers to her as she.

I had forgotten so many details about the place – that, from the outside, it looks like a disused garden shed, that it has no hot water, no heat at all, and that Lucy bathes herself in the garden with a hose, even in winter. She heats the place with a wood-burning stove, and cooks by moving pots and pans on and off the heat. The toilet is next to the sink, and there is nothing but a little saloon-style swinging door separating you from anyone else in the house. The ground floor is no more than ten feet by fifteen feet, and there's a bedroom upstairs with a small balcony, from which, at night, when you can see the lights, Vienna blinks like a vast metropolis, even though it is not one. She has decorated it, inside, with an impressive collection of kitsch and costume jewellery and pictures of herself. And yet, with all this kitsch and decay, there is an atmosphere of delicacy and elegance about the place – though perhaps this comes only from her. In the basement, there is a cold room full of hundreds of bottles of vodka, which she can drink like lemonade.

Lucy made us tea, and we listened to an interview of her that played recently on ORF. And then some live recordings of her in various venues around the world. She cooked us some salmon and salad, and we ate around her little couch. She has an extremely smooth and deep voice that could put you to sleep if it did not say so many outrageously filthy things. I sat with my back to the window, but opposite a gigantic vanity mirror where she applies make-up and puts on wigs and jewellery, and – for the nights she is to entertain, or stand on stage, or sing, or DJ – transforms herself into a woman of such unquantifiable beauty that heterosexual men buy her nonsensically expensive presents in the hope of sleeping with her. The salmon was simple but full of flavour. I could not believe she cooked anything – there was no empty surface to work on. She seemed to do all her preparation in the air. After a while we took a walk around her garden, which slopes down fifty yards or so. In the spring and summer you can barely walk through it, because it is so overgrown, but in winter you can see the underlying order. Half of her plants are poisonous, and that is precisely the way she thinks of herself. Walter asked her for some gardening tips, since he plans to do some rearranging of his parents' garden this year.

Slowly we said our goodbyes – we will see her again on Thursday at Motto, where she DJs once a month. Walter seemed a bit more relaxed after our hours of tea, conversation, and walks in the garden. We went home and Walter slept for an hour – his ten days off because of his neck had come to an end, and he had to be in work the next morning. We had dinner reservations at eight-thirty, so Walter and I went to St Peter's Church for the free twenty-minute organ concert at eight. We sat in the back row. Clare and I had done this when she was here, but in the afternoon. The church was dark, except for orange spotlights shooting through the dome, and candles burning around us. The organist played a fugue by Bach. When we walked out Walter breathed very deeply through his nose. That night, after dinner and a few drinks at the bar up the road, I came home and listened to some Bach that Walter recommended – cello and violin suites. I went to bed and played it on my headphones until I fell asleep.

Walter left for work this morning – it is Monday – and at lunchtime, after the first few hours of work, he sent me a text saying his neck was as bad as it had been ten days ago, and that he was at the doctor's.

I set out early in a kind of grey rain-snow with my headphones. It has been so many days since I've read a book that my German is starting to regress. I don't watch television apart from the skiing, because Walter likes to watch it – and now seven weeks have gone by since I even glanced at a newspaper. I left Walter sitting in his kitchen smoking cigarettes and drinking tea. His head had once again sunk into his chest, and he had not slept because of the pain.

I took the U4 to Karlsplatz but took the exit to Bösendorfer-strasse and bought some CDs at Haus der Musik. After that, I only wanted to walk around some of the empty narrow streets and exorcize language from my appreciation of Bach, to continue to rearrange the way my brain studied music. This was impossible. Thoughts came raining out of the back of my brain. I wished I could reach in through my mouth and extract them. When I leave, and there is only the permanent self of my past in Vienna, I would like to think that he, that self, may exist in a condition of sound and sight alone, a figure in gloomy weather, sunshine, night, and snow.

I hiked up to Schloss Belvedere, first around the grounds that face Upper Belvedere. There were only three other people there, and they were taking photos of each other taking photos of each other with three different cameras. I walked around the large, empty fountain, then down through the gardens toward Lower Belvedere. The gardens are being revitalized, according to small displays staged all around the paths as a sort of apology. There was nobody around but some Asian tourists and a few construction workers smoking cigarettes around bits of dug-up earth. Beyond Lower Belvedere, Stephansdom was looming hazily above the centre of the city – and somehow with the sight was the implication of all my comings and goings there, and my dispensability. But these words come now; when I saw the tower flashing in and out of the blowing-sideways haze, I merely felt like I had seen what I had come to see. My Bach ran out, and I felt it would ruin the experience to play it again.

And now I am sitting in Kleines Café beside a beautiful Taiwanese woman and an ugly, short American man. It is impossible not to eavesdrop, because they are speaking in English – I have surmised that she is a professional concert violinist and he is a struggling, broke, untalented violinist. She is about to start a tour of Asia, and he tells her he is getting old and has no accomplishments. What's an accomplishment? she asks. Something you do that you can make a career out of, he says. I have been here for an hour and he has done nothing but complain. He has a voice that is just one octave away from crying. The waitress brings him a Melange – in Kleines Café the Melange comes with a large amount of whipped milk on top – and he says, like a little child who has lost his toy, in a German that is brutally Americanized in accent, But I ordered my Melange *without* whipped cream. (Aburr ick habbuh meinuh muhlonj *ohne* schlawg buhshtellt.) She says, irascibly, that it's not whipped cream, but milk – that's the way it is served. Okay, he sighs – that sigh could have killed a thousand sunflowers on a hillside. And then he tells the Taiwanese girl that he needs to reduce his fat intake, and milk has a lot of fat. Send it back, the girl says. No, he says. Never mind. Sighing again. He says he has trouble with women because he respects them too much. It is good to respect women, she says. He tells her he does not have the patience to practise music and study it at the same time. She says it is necessary, if one is to become a musician. He is bald but lets his hair grow out at the sides and back, and a little patch at the top. She has long black hair and wears a white jumper. She is the most beautiful girl I have seen in days. She moves her empty espresso cup around impatiently. The complaints go on and on. His posture is hunched and ashamed. Today, he says, all he could do was clean the floor of his apartment, which is small, and which he hates. Well, she says – and what is she supposed to say? – cleaning your apartment can be therapeutic. He shrugs. There is a girl he likes, but she doesn't like to meet on weekdays, only on weekends, and she gets too drunk. You should teach her how to enjoy weekdays, she says. No, no, I can't. I don't want to change anyone. If I love someone, I must respect her decisions. I want to haul him up by his collar and toss him through the window. To have this beautiful woman in front of him and despair. To complain away the hour. To blame women for his shame – to blame respect for his distaste of them. Perhaps he thinks she will take pity on him, love him for the sweetness he wears to conceal his identity, the envying, hating, self-pitying man whose only sincere realization is that he wants more than he can have. And he has turned this into a philosophy. The things he said! About reading that having positive thoughts led to success, except that he could have no positive thoughts. The fact that his bow was responsible for the sick sounds that came out of his violin. You should buy a new bow, she says. But I have no money, he says. No wonder you won't make a musician, I want to say. I want to break my chair over his back, throw him through the window and strangle him in the street. And then take his place opposite the violinist and say, Let's start over.

I got back to the house very late that evening, and even though I'd had a lot to drink I was not drunk. I sat in the kitchen and played Bach again – partita for guitar – on Walter's little stereo: for some reason this was the music that Walter was listening to most. Then I played some Vivaldi. I closed the kitchen door so I could listen with the volume up: I was drunk and tired, and this helped me appreciate the music without much thought. When I go back to Dublin, I know that I will play this music quietly over dinners and while working; it will drift into the background. Here, in Walter's apartment, I remove distractions. I do nothing I can set to music; the music is all that there is. I poured a glass of wine and drank under a dim red lamp. And when I came very close to something I cannot describe at all, a proximity to the music that felt almost like a possession, I shook my head clear. All this would be gone in ten days. I staggered into my bedroom, pulled off my jeans and shoes and wrestled the shirt off me, and slept. When I woke, at ten, the snow was roaring past my window.

An afternoon at Christl and Erich's – the friends I spent New Year's Eve with. They are in their sixties, but you wouldn't notice. I woke up around eleven, after taking my first night off drink since early December, and I had never felt so tired. My body was sore and stiff. I had black circles under my eyes and felt nauseated. But my mind was a little more awake. The hot water was gone because it was so late, so I filled the bath with lukewarm water, then boiled four large pots on the stove and tossed the boiling water in. I put on Scriabin and Glazunov, and, through the open bathroom door, through the corridor, through my room, I watched the snow float down like fat feathers. It had snowed all night, and it was supposed to snow all day, and the next.

I met Walter after a trip to the doctor – he receives an infusion and massage therapy every day. He was not doing well. He was doing, in fact, much worse. I asked him how the appointment went. He said the therapist – not the regular therapist, but someone new – had grown frustrated because he could not relax, and he had cried for half an hour. The therapist left him alone, and he had cried on his own – and he had no idea why. It was something he could not identify. Something *Existenz*, he said. The uncertainty was making him worse by the minute. We took the bus as far as we could take it – Walter was in no condition to walk the half-hour up the hills to Baumgarten. We stepped out at a large cemetery. It was pure white – the hillsides rolling upward on one side of us, and the white graves rolling downward on the other. By the time we got to Christl and Erich's, Walter couldn't get his coat off.

Christl and Erich live in a large house that is curiously decorated and very cold. It is grey, black, and white, and the abstract
art on the walls is very dark, morose, and sexual: greys, maroons,
browns. There are also shelves full of strange collectibles:
hundreds of little ink pots, or sugar dispensers, and, in the stair-
well, on the window sill and on two large tables, thousands of
weights, from the size of an ant up. I thought I'd heard from
Walter that they sleep in separate bedrooms, but Christl showed
me a room on the second floor with a futon and a shelf with a
stereo and a bunch of untidy CDs. This is where she and Erich
go, she said, when they want to be like poor students who live
on music and passion.

They made a large lunch for us. I was forced to eat two full
plates of food and drink a beer, even though my stomach was
upside down. They gave Walter three glasses of diluted magne-
sium for his neck, and forced him to lie down on a magnetic-field
bed for eight minutes – no more, no less. Walter and I asked what
a magnetic-field bed was, and Christl explained, but I didn't
understand the explanation. Erich is the kind of man who makes
me feel inferior: he builds. He takes things apart and puts them
back together. He bought the house next door, which was full
of trash, emptied it, and renovated it – but Christl loves the
garden behind so much that she won't let him rent it out. He
landscaped that garden, built a giant garage by himself, and put
a swimming pool in the basement of his own house. He let me
see a few rooms in the house next door in which he stores
hundreds of model ships and airplanes. And later, when Christl
and Walter were inside having a second cup of coffee, Erich took
me to a spot in his garden, which was under large evergreens
covered in snow, to show me some sculptures he created – large

stones somehow fastened to small steel foundations. He simply found the stones beautiful, and wanted to make art out of them. I agreed they were beautiful, and that presenting them in the way he did made art out of them. Yes, he said, that is what I did.

Christl is also an eccentric. If she had had a daughter, she would have been one of those mothers who is much more fun than the daughter, and disappointed by the daughter's seriousness. Every story you tell her, she retells to all her friends for eternity, as though it is the most interesting thing that ever happened. She finds it endearing that Erich is a hound dog when it comes to other women, and, in a tour of the house, laughed at all the evidence of his obsession with large breasts. She gave me, as a present, the shirt they put her son in the day he was born, and which has been passed down many generations.

Erich gave us a lift home, since the snow was getting worse, and Walter had deteriorated. We had a concert in the Musikverein that night, a French string quartet playing in the Brahms Saal: Mozart, Bartók, and Dvořák. Erich dropped us off at the Testarellogasse bridge. We got out, and a woman in a long black coat walked by. It was dark by then, but she was lit by the bright windows of an office building beside us. She had long black hair and dark eyes. She glanced at me and then away. I watched her walk away from me. She was beautiful, I told Walter. Walter said, Yes, I've never seen a woman so beautiful.

I am writing now in the mid-afternoon. My hands are trembling and I am in the thick of a cold sweat. I have had half a dozen cups of coffee and a bowl of fruit. I am thinking of naked bodies. I am thinking of Maxine's legs, of her on stage in Linz today. I am thinking of my hand on Astrid's ass, of lying in bed with her and her sister. I imagine Clare at home with a finger inside herself, coming, thinking of what we will get up to when I return. It's always like this when I am hungover.

I am not in the best condition to write, but last night may slip away from me if I do not record it, and John arrives in three hours. I shall try to do it some justice. After the concert, Walter and I went to Motto to see Lucy DJ. Motto is a mixed bar not far from the U4 station Pilgramgasse. I had never seen so many beautiful women, nor so many gay men in white shirts and slicked-back black hair and sunglasses. The bar was dark and violet. Lucy was wearing a tight black dress and red wig. We sat down at the bar beside two women. One was blonde, tall, and wore shorts over black tights and purple boots; the other was short and round and black-haired and looked a bit like Joan Jett. I smiled at the blonde girl when I first arrived, and she turned her head and pulled her hair down. But later, Lucy introduced us: the blonde was Maxine, the black-haired girl was Barbara. Lucy told them I was from Texas but lived in Ireland. Barbara said, in English, Where in Ireland?

Dublin, I said.

Never been there, she said. Never been to Ireland. I'm from London.

You're from London, and you've never been to Dublin?

Darling, I've never been to parts of north London.

Barbara was a singer and actress, and knew Lucy from a show they'd done together. Maxine, who is Viennese, leaned over and said: She's very good – a wonderful singer. Lucy agreed – she said Barbara's voice gives you an erection, though she said so indirectly and very politely. They were on the way out, but Maxine said I could buy her a drink. We chatted for a while. Carolin arrived, and Walter spoke with her while I spoke to Maxine and Barbara.

Maxine was staring at me. She had very clear blue eyes. Even when Barbara was speaking to her, she stared at me. I went to the bathroom to check that there was nothing wrong with my face. The urinal at Motto is a wall-high mirror so that men can see each other's dicks. An old man stood beside me and stared. It's very large, he said. Thank you, I said.

It's also circumcised, and very pretty.

I suppose, I said, shaking it for him.

Would you like me to suck it?

No thanks, I said.

I returned to Maxine. I lied about how big my going-away party would be the next weekend. In truth I imagined that only Walter, Lucy and one or two others would come if I asked. Barbara left for a moment, and it was just me and Maxine, and she turned to me and crossed her legs. I asked her to stay for a few more drinks, but she was tired and had rehearsals in the morning. She gave me her number. She would gladly make the *Abschiedsparty*. Let's do it in Motto, she said. That's the smartest, I said – now I was speaking in German again.

Over the hour or two since we'd arrived, I'd had about five shots of vodka – most of them placed in front of my face by Lucy, who seemed to have one every five minutes. She also drank gin, soda and cucumber. She liked the suitability of gin and cucumber, she said, though cucumber would probably be just as suitable with vodka. Then she clapped her hands – but clapped is not the word, more like slowly glued them together – and smiled: *Apropos vodka!* And another shot was put in front of me. She played a folksy Austrian tune that everyone knew the words to, and everyone stopped trying to look sophisticated for a moment and sang along.

When Maxine stood to leave, and I kissed her, she had two inches on me – without heels. She stooped a little, and I stood a bit on my tiptoes, and we kissed each other's cheeks. Then Walter left. He said he wasn't having any fun, because he felt so awkward, and he could not drink because of his medication. Carolin followed half an hour later. And I was on my own, at least until Lucy played her last number – which would be two a.m. I moved a seat closer to two blonde girls – not natural blondes, and clearly sisters – and eavesdropped. I could not make out a single word, nothing I could use to drop myself into the conversation, until I realized they were speaking English; once I adjusted my ears to English I heard everything. They were Irish. I introduced myself: You're Irish, I said.

The older sister said, That's right.

I live in Dublin, I said.

The older sister was Alex, the younger was Astrid. Alex lived in Vienna, Astrid lived in Australia, but they were from Galway. And – who knows how these things happen – two hours later I was standing close to Astrid in a gay nightclub called Mango. Astrid was sitting beside Lucy, who was pickled – her word – half sleeping, sometimes managing the energy to flirt with random men, or sign an autograph, and every now and again to quote some famous line from some famous female singer or movie star from the fifties, or from Dean Martin. Astrid told me she was married, and a few minutes later she admitted she was eight weeks pregnant. We drank beer and shots until six in the morning. Alex was trying to kiss a 23-year-old bartender from Motto. There was an asshole there with a black leather jacket who grabbed Astrid's tits in the ladies' toilet, and an hour later grabbed Alex's tits at the bar, right in front of me, and suddenly I felt like a fight. I wanted to beat his brains in. I grabbed him by the collar and tossed him outside. I threw him on the pavement. Astrid and a few others grabbed me and pulled me back. The asshole tried to get back inside. I met him at the door and threw him back out on the street. The bartender – a tiny little gay boy who looked like he might break if you squeezed him – asked me to go back to the bar. No problem, I said. Then he told the asshole that he was banned, forever. I'll be waiting here for you, the asshole shouted at me. Give me half an hour, I shouted back. Astrid and I drank some more shots and Lucy said, *My hero*. And when I looked around again everyone seemed to be kissing, men and women, men and men, men and boys, boys and boys. Except for Lucy. Lucy does not kiss. She gets up to the filthiest things imaginable, but she does not kiss.

When we left the bar at six, the Irish girls had no money, and no bank cards. They needed twenty euro for a taxi. I suggested we all get a taxi home together and have a threesome. Then suddenly they were arguing about whose fault it was that they had stayed out so late. Astrid was leaving for Sydney the next day, and Alex had to work at nine. I couldn't tell if the argument was serious or a joke, but I wanted no part of it. I kissed them goodbye, gave them some money, and caught the U4 at Pilgramgasse. I got on the rearmost carriage, and because it was a new train, with an open gangway from back to front, I made my way stumbling and swaying and rebalancing and excusing myself to the front. I believe I prepared myself something to eat when I got home, but this may not have happened. Walter got out of bed to go to the bathroom. *Hallihallo*, he said, sleepily, in his little white underwear. I put my headphones on and played Mompou's *Variations on a Theme by Chopin*.

I picked John up at Landstrasse, where you catch the express train to the airport. It was about eight p.m. He had packed light for the weekend: a phone and two shirts, a change of underwear, and some socks. He asked about our plans for the evening, and I said it was dinner and drinks with Walter, but that things were not going well with Walter, and he might not come out at all. When John and I arrived, Walter was drunk, so he was doing a little better. He had turned all the lights off and lit all the candles in the apartment, and was listening to a collection of famous arias.

After a brief dinner in Naschmarkt, Walter led us around the southern edge of the First District, by Karlskirche, then Schwarzenbergplatz, because he wanted to take us to Peter's Operncafé, the place where he had spent his twenties. It was a wet and cold night. The Ring was busy with taxis, but once we crossed into the First District there was just a strange cool emptiness. *Madama Butterfly* was playing – someone other than Callas. I realized at once that this was the place Christian, the boss at Santo Spirito, meant when he told me, one evening a few weeks back, to go down the road if I wanted to listen to Puccini. Walter explained that the two bars have something of a hatred for each other – but a respectful hatred. Peter's Operncafé was where all the important players in operas went for drinks after opening nights. Peter himself, an older gay man who wore, that night, a sleeveless muscle shirt and moved around the café as though he were on ice skates, has such high standards when it comes to opera and considers himself such a pivotal figure in the opera scene – the singers ask him for his autograph, for instance – that he is obligated to hate everything. I asked him what he thought of Netrebko, and he nearly fainted with dismay. He put the back of his hand to his forehead and wobbled. Walter used to go there by himself in the afternoons and sit at the bar and listen to music, and ask Peter who was who and what was what. The walls are covered in portraits of opera greats. Peter has told Walter the story behind every picture. Half the stories are true, says Walter.

John said: Fuck me, horse, this is a cool place.

I wished I had known about it sooner. To think that I had let so many afternoons and evenings go by in search of a place exactly like this – and I had only a week left.

John and I had three beers each, and Walter had two. Peter hadn't seen Walter in years, so he played a few arias especially for us – 'Nessun dorma' (Walter wanted us to enjoy it like he enjoyed it: it was a pity that John recognized it as the theme music from Italia '90), 'La vita è inferno', 'Vissi d'arte' (I had said I'd seen *Tosca*, and he said he'd introduce me to a version worth listening to), and some others Walter wasn't quite sure about. From time to time, the conversation would stop. Walter would close his eyes and lean his head back, or conduct with one finger, and I would look up at the ceiling.

Later we left for Santo Spirito. We got the last free table, just by the stairs that lead down from the entrance. Christian was working, and he and Walter said hello. Then some other men greeted Walter – it had been a long time, I realized, since he'd seen anybody. John said, Is everybody in Vienna gay? Walter said, The best way to be introduced to Vienna is the gay way.

Is the scene good here? John asked. I believe it's shit in Dublin.

Walter said, It's a little better than it used to be. In fact, it was because of Walter and a dozen others that there's a scene at all. During his twenties and early thirties, Walter had been part of a group that opened Café Berg – now an institution – and Heaven, which was Thursday nights at the nightclub U4, and Bar X. These had sparked the scene.

Christian played a few things I did not know, then the projection screen rolled down and we watched a film of Karajan directing the New Year's Day Concert – waltzes from Strauss. Then some other pieces – Walter kept asking me to name the composer, and usually I couldn't, though a few times he said I was close. But I identified Beethoven. During the Beethoven, Walter sat with his legs crossed and his eyes closed, and when it was over, he opened his eyes and sighed. It's a special treat to get 'Ode to Joy' in Santo, I told John. John said he never thought he'd hear such a strange sentence in his life. And then Christian brought us some schnapps. During our time there, John and I had some conversations I cannot remember – but I remember that Walter interrupted to say he was shocked that we had the ability to think so logically and objectively about our subjects. He said he can never think logically about anything – he has no ability to solve problems; he is always struck dumb by everything. But which was better – to talk nonsense for an hour, or to experience music like he could? I told him I was jealous. Walter considered this for a moment, then said, That's nice; thank you.

The next day started late – John and I had managed to stay out drinking until seven in the morning. We left the apartment around lunchtime and had a club sandwich and a beer each at the Kunsthalle Café. I was starting to get used to the women in Vienna, but having John around changed my perspective. We would sometimes have to stop a conversation to ask each other, You did see that, right? I took him to the Leopold Museum to see the Schiele collection. I had fierce indigestion at this point, and left him to it – I sat on the toilet for half an hour. I knew then that I would have to start drinking immediately if I wanted to feel better, and that this would ruin Sunday – we were supposed to go see Lucy on Sunday – but there was no choice now. There was nothing to do but finish it.

I led him through the Imperial Palace and told him the story about the artist responsible for the statue of the horse on two legs. I was told the story when I was fifteen, and it is so far-fetched I don't believe it – that the artist was killed after he finished, so that nowhere else would have a statue like it – but I continue to tell it to everyone I have brought to Vienna over the years, and even sometimes to the Viennese. Then a few hours in Alt Wien. I know most of the waiters by sight now, and they know me by sight, so we greeted each other warmly. We ordered some beer and decided to begin our drinking in earnest – this was around three p.m. When I told John I was writing the last chapter of my book, he congratulated me. He said I was a different man. He had never seen me looking so certain in my disregard for small things. I told him he was right: I had never felt so pointless. I spent two years extracting all the lies out of my past, setting fire to them – eradicating, as much as it is possible, an identity of falsehood, jealousy, betrayal, and cowardice: a warped and selfish adaptation to the expectations of others. And I had replaced it, until I got here, with nothing at all. I had retreated from intent. I had retreated from others. Michi says this is impossible – that a retreat is, at the very least, still a position. John said, when I told him that: Fine, but what the fuck do you call such a position? What do you call a position that won't stay still, and won't engage in an argument? Exactly, I said. In order to think of it as a position you must redefine *position*. And when you begin to redefine terms to make sense of things outside the world of terms you use to grasp reality, you are lying again.

But in this vacuum of intent, in my refusal to accept an identity in language – an identity in grammar – here, in Vienna, through Walter, I was filling it with mornings and afternoons in the apartment, listening to music. Or concerts. Or Santo Spirito. And I was approaching – not often, but often enough to appreciate the possibility of it in Walter – an appreciation of music outside the articulable. And this had moved into the space where before there was nothing but lies, and ambition, and envy.

Later that night, after dinner, we met some girls I knew. One of the girls, who cornered John, forced him into a conversation about Northern Ireland, and this – along with the alcohol – made him paranoid for the rest of the night. No one I ever met is more interesting to talk to than John, when he is sober or a little drunk, but when he gets very drunk he turns into Hunter S. Thompson. Everything gives him the grim. He made me ditch the girls because they didn't like him – which was pure fantasy – and we went back to Santo Spirito, then to Loos Bar until four. I left him alone at both bars for long stretches because the indigestion was coming back, and when I returned he said, Horse, let's get the fuck out of here; these fuckers are watching me. The next day, Sunday, was a dark day. I woke up and watched, for the second time, *La Bohème* on DVD, with Netrebko, and I wept. I had the grim myself. John lay in bed all day and watched a movie on his phone, a bad Hollywood film, and the end made him weep. He threw up in a bag I was using for dirty clothes, and some of it leaked onto the bed and floor. This happened just at the moment Walter and I were beginning to try to eat some carrot and ginger soup. And when I returned from taking him to the airport, Walter left the apartment for a few hours to walk around the city and contemplate committing suicide.

I do not exist, he says. I have never existed. We are in his living room now, in darkness, listening to Beethoven – Piano Sonata

No. 8. He is drifting in and out of a connection with it. I am trying to say nothing. I have no future, he says. No hope. I have nothing to wake up for, except to go to therapy for my neck. I could die tomorrow and nothing would change. He is smoking one cigarette after the other, and I have lit a little candle for him. Everyone I know has ambition, he says. They live with goals. They have real jobs, or they are artists. Except, when they talk, they say nothing but shit, nonsense.

Walter starts drinking the moment he wakes up. He has a joint with a coffee. He will drink all day. Otherwise he cannot stand the sound of people speaking. Otherwise he will spend every moment contemplating his inexistence, his unimportance, and for him this is horror. Without cocaine he can't leave the house at night – this is an admission that he has started again. He has tried to commit suicide twice. He says he is once again on the edge. The thought of ending his life – which he'd contemplated on the long walk in the city – has eased the pain in his neck. The act of suicide is an act: he can decide, he has control, and this is a kind of future.

The room is filling with smoke. The smoke seems to be made of music. And now it is Chopin's Piano Concerto No. 1, the 'Romanza', and for ten minutes we say nothing at all. He seems to levitate off the old orange-brown sofa. It is as though the music is made of little strings that wrap around his limbs and waist, his fingers, his toes, the backs of his knees, and his neck, and lift him. A free man, finally a man who is free. I will never experience music like he does. The chemistry that holds him together is made of a radically unstable substance – sound. And it is either in perfect harmony or it is in disharmony. When it is in disharmony, drugs hold him together. Everyone around him exists in the regulated half-harmony of everydayness; they are manners of living. But he is a thing, not a manner. Infinitely persuadable, infinitely usable. And in his gradual recognition of this weakness he has reduced the once-magnificent circle of his associations to two or three people. A free man, with the rarest and highest form of intelligence – an instinct for meaning. To approach this understanding I gave up reading. I set aside all influence but music. And occasionally there has been, in these last days, a pure connection, unfiltered by language, sitting in his living room, alone, with all the lights off, and I can only explain it in metaphor: it is like opening your eyes in black water. It is like putting your head through the surface of a deep black lake, and sinking all the way to your waist, and you are naked above the waist, and opening your eyes – there is nothing; there are no shapes; there is no light; there are no voices. There is only the water, which is the music itself. And the experience is so terrifying to the mind – because it is so near death – that the mind throws language around your neck to pull you out. Walter somehow exists in this nightmare. If I had the courage to keep my eyes open, and drift down a long way, I would find Walter there, floating near a light that he has found.

A friend, Daniela, gave me an old violin case as a going-away present. Six weeks ago I joked that I wanted to have a violin case to walk around the city with, so that people would think I was a musician. She knows an old man who is a musician, and he said there was an old case in his attic. People are reluctant to give up antique violin cases, because they can be quite valuable, but Daniela persuaded him. She will not tell me how, but I presume she gave him quite a bit of money. And for a night I got to walk around Vienna with a violin case. Of course, the Viennese would know it was a joke – nobody uses old cases – but for the few tourists here in February, I might have become an occasion for remembrance, a man in a bar sitting beside his violin after a concert he had given. And I'm the girl in a hat with the musician, said Daniela.

I have started to get very tired. Perhaps it was the three nights out till morning, or perhaps it is the thought of returning to Dublin. Of the last glimpses of an impossible life. I hear it is snowing in Dublin, but it has been warm and grey in Vienna for the past week. I walk around with my pea coat open. Walter has made a decision to go into rehab – a last shot at existence, he says; the day after I leave, he will go to a clinic to live clean for a few months. He has also been diagnosed with depression. I did some shopping for Clare and got some lederhosen for our baby. I also bought a little blue winter cap for when he is born. The size of it in my hands, there in the shop on Kärtnerstrasse, and again on the street with Walter outside a music shop, is the first experience I have had in which his arrival – in a few months – seems almost real.

In 2002, on my second-to-last night in Vienna, a bunch of us got together in Onka's restaurant, to celebrate the end of my four weeks. Christl and Erich were there. So was Daniela. Walter was there, and his brother Michael, and some other friends. A few of the staff stayed around after the bar closed. Onka played music until four a.m., and when everyone left, Walter, Onka, Michael and I remained. Onka suggested we get a taxi to the Jubiläumswarte – a lookout tower – in the hills on the edge of the city, and watch the sun come up over Vienna. She took a few bottles of champagne out of a refrigerator. The drive there lasted half an hour, because we got a little lost, and there was already light in the sky. We climbed up the spiral staircase hurriedly. This was the first or second day of July. A heatwave had been raging for weeks. The sky above the city was hazy. Before the sun came up, the city was grey-blue – and we sat together with our legs hanging over the edge for half an hour, drinking. When the sun cracked the horizon, the grey-blue was vaporized by gold, a gold so dramatic that it burned our eyes. There had been a lot of talking before that, but suddenly there was nothing to be said. Michael put his hand on my shoulder. We stayed there for another hour, and Walter fell asleep.

This time, Walter and I had planned to drive an hour out of town to another lookout tower, but in the mountains. But with all the tumult caused by his worsening condition and his departure next week, this plan has been abandoned. Tonight I am meeting Christl and Erich, Daniela, Dieter and Heidi – and perhaps Walter will join us – at a gallery opening near Urban Loritz Platz, and then we will go to a restaurant in the Eighth District. Maybe Daniela and I will stay out late. I have kept tomorrow free for myself. I will have my headphones, and plan to walk around the city all day – fog is the forecast for the morning, then sunshine. I may walk to the Votivkirche. I will visit the Schiele exhibit alone. Tomorrow night, after a dinner by myself, I will go to Peter's Operncafé and listen to some music. When I get home, I will have a bottle of wine in the kitchen and listen to some of the new music Walter and I bought. And at some point during this day I plan to separate the self I shall leave here from the self that will return: to cast the author of this book into a condition of permanent aimlessness, here in Vienna. I will go one direction and he will go another. This is my wish for him, since, if he returns to Dublin, he will forget the perfection of inexistence. He will grow out of the despair he worships. I cannot send him back to an office. I cast him into darkness. May he haunt the lives of the characters here as long as they live. May I glimpse him one day when I return.

On Saturday, my last night, I will meet some members of the old fraternity – Walter, Lucy, a half-dozen others – at Santo Spirito, and later we're meeting Maxine and Barbara at Motto: they are back from Linz for the weekend. Sunday, I will pack up and go. Walter's also going to pack. Dieter and Heidi will take me to the airport. We will wish we had longer. This is always the way at the airport – not enough has been said; not enough has been done.

So the end exists not here, not now, but in the empty, unlived space of the next few days.

Acknowledgements

Special thanks to Brendan Barrington.

Financial assistance from The Arts Council of Ireland is gratefully acknowledged.

Versions of 'Two Working Days', 'That Lovely Season Now Expired', 'The City of Perpetual Night' and 'Glitter Gulch' first appeared in *The Dublin Review*.